Managing Sustainability

Managing Sustainability

First Steps to First Class

John Friedman

BUSINESS EXPERT PRESS

First published in 2020 by
Business Expert Press, LLC
222 East 46th Street, New York, NY 10017
www.businessexpertpress.com

ISBN-13: 978-1-95152-774-7 (paperback)
ISBN-13: 978-1-95152-775-4 (e-book)

Business Expert Press Environmental and Social Sustainability for Business Advantage Collection

Collection ISSN: 2327-333X (print)
Collection ISSN: 2327-3348 (electronic)

Cover photo courtesy of Interior Plantscapes, Laurel, MD
Cover and interior design by S4Carlisle Publishing Services Private Ltd., Chennai, India

First edition: 2020

10 9 8 7 6 5 4 3 2 1

Printed in the United States of America.

Abstract

Sustainability professionals or business strategists who are seeking to integrate effective programs that match corporate strategy with the purpose and values-driven initiatives that engage employees, build customer loyalty, and improve license to operate will benefit from the author's more than 30 years' experience in corporate communications, business, and corporate sustainability.

Managing Sustainability: First Steps to First Class provides a compelling case, real-world examples, and the tools to follow a proven strategy for aligning sustainability efforts with existing organizational priorities. This strategy has taken companies from initial conception to the top of the DJSI/RobecoSAM and MSCI sustainability rankings in three very different business sectors: construction, materials, food services and facilities management, and energy. Using examples from these and other leading companies, readers will understand the importance of creating—and more importantly how to build—programs that drive results and enhance reputation.

Benefits include enabling companies to attract, hire, retain, and (most importantly) fully engage the best talent, seize the innovation high ground with new and premium products and services, provide access to an ever-increasing pool of socially responsible investment capital, implement "best practices," earn social license to operate, reduce compliance and regulatory costs, and more.

The methodology described includes the latest trend (and increasing expectation) to go beyond the organization's own "footprint" to integrate their values into their supply chains and build employee and customer loyalty by empowering these essential stakeholders to live their shared values.

Keywords

business strategy; strategic alignment; sustainability; corporate responsibility; best practices; organizational excellence; results; reputation; leadership; management; employee engagement; environment; social; governance; ESG; sustainable development goals, SDGs

Contents

Foreword

Our home, planet Earth, is roughly four and a half billion years old. When we, as human beings, think about our lives, our work, our legacy, and those who will come after us, we like to imagine that this world will go on forever. We hope that an infinite number of generations will continue to come along and enjoy the same beauty, the same prosperity, and the same expectations of a better future brimming with wonderful possibilities.

That vision is at the heart of sustainability.

In this book, *Managing Sustainability: First Steps to First Class*, author John Friedman examines the role of business in forging such a world.

A practitioner of the aspiring art of "corporate social responsibility," Friedman takes a no-nonsense look at the several meanings of sustainability in the commercial sector. After all, making money, growing a customer base, and, at the heart of it all, staying in business are the very core of sustainability in the business world.

However, in a larger sense, people today believe that the vision of a sustainable future includes them. It is an expectation of societies around the world, written into law by governments everywhere. Business is duty bound to be a proper steward of social fairness, equal opportunity, and environmental responsibility. We expect our executives to be examples of moral rectitude. Just ask any (former) higher-up out of work for reasons of personal conduct, especially in the #MeToo era.

What the author addresses so articulately in this book is the necessary next step that follows from corporate social responsibility, that is, creating shared value.

Those of us who teach business in the 21st century tell our students that—yes—it is your imperative to make money and stay in business. But it is also an imperative to preserve and enhance the world from which you draw your wealth.

That obligation, this new "sustainability," includes principles of fairness, expanded opportunity for striving peoples fighting obstacles of disadvantage of all kinds, and, so importantly, preserving and raising the quality of our home, planet Earth.

Louise L. Schiavone
Johns Hopkins University Carey Business School
Baltimore, MD

CHAPTER 1

Introduction

Corporate Sustainability

For many people the concept of "sustainability"—meeting the needs of this generation while safeguarding those of generations to come—is synonymous with environmental protection and stewardship. However, those working in the space focus on three main pillars: economic, environmental, and social. This is what starts to separate an effort to balance or meet all three needs with "environmentalism."

For businesses, the term "corporate sustainability" is broken into three related but slightly different categories: environment, social, and governance (ESG)—the concept being that much of what a business does economically has to be done ethically, transparently, and with proper checks and balances in place. For the purposes of this book, the term "sustainability" relies on the later definition because it is also focused on the need for the business to sustain, as well as the environment and the societies/communities in which it operates.

One need only to look back a decade to the Great Recession and the collapse of the global housing market to see an example of unsustainable economic business practices. There were many reasons for the collapse, which was primarily caused by a rise in subprime mortgage lending (selling housing loans to people with poor credit) and a massive increase in housing prices. Riding the wave up were financial institutions, regulators, credit agencies, and consumers (who did not want to miss out on easy credit and often did not understand the terms of the loans that they were being sold) as well as those who took advantage of the "easy money" to be made by buying and selling (flipping) houses while prices spiraled upward.

In 2015, the Environmental Protection Agency (EPA) discovered that Volkswagen had been cheating in emissions tests by intentionally programming some of its vehicles to activate their emissions controls only during emissions testing, but to release up to 40 times the legal limits during real-world driving. The EPA determined that the cheating affected about 500,000 cars in America and 11 million worldwide. Regulators in multiple countries began to investigate the company and its stock price fell in value by a third in the days immediately after the news. Volkswagen Group CEO Martin Winterkorn resigned. Volkswagen announced plans in April 2016 to spend €16.2 billion (US$18.32 billion) to refit the affected vehicles as part of a recall campaign. In 2017, Volkswagen pleaded guilty to criminal charges and the company was ordered to pay a $2.8 billion criminal fine.

Perhaps the most tragic recent example of how the pillars interact was on April 24, 2013, when the Rana Plaza building in Bangladesh collapsed, killing more than a thousand underpaid garment workers producing clothing for fast fashion retailers such as H&M and Zara. Workers' complaints about the building security had been ignored on multiple occasions, and the day before the tragedy, cracks were discovered on the lower floors of the building, but the management decided to ignore the warnings.

Why One Needs the Three Pillars

Sustainability is distinct in that it works to find solutions that balance (or meet) the three "pillars." Making decisions that overbalance one (i.e., economic) can all too easily sacrifice the others. Focusing purely on even the most idealistic goals can lead to decisions that are grounded more in emotion than on facts. The imperative to address climate change is real, but focusing only on the promise of "renewable electricity," as an example, can lead to some well-intended efforts with unintended consequences. The US Energy Information Agency (EIA) projects strong growth for wind and solar power in the United States, so that the total share of U.S. electricity generation produced by all renewables other than hydropower will increase from 10 percent of total generation in 2018 to 13 percent in 2020.[1]

---

[1]US EIA. 2019. "EIA Forecasts Renewables Will Be Fastest Growing Source of Electricity Generation." https://www.eia.gov/todayinenergy/detail.php?id=38053, (accessed October 12, 2019).

What this means is that fossil fuels will still provide most of the electricity generated in the United States. Coal and natural gas combined provided 63 percent of electricity generation in 2018 and EIA forecasts that they will provide 61 percent in 2020.

In fact, most of the greenhouse gas reductions in the United States have been due to the shift of U.S. electricity away from coal toward natural gas, which has grown faster than renewables. The EIA forecasts that this trend will continue, meaning that efforts to "keep it in the ground" run into the stark reality that the U.S. economy and the health and well-being of millions of people rely on doing the exact opposite and will for decades to come, absent major technological breakthroughs in both renewable generation and storage.

In October 2019, wildfires forced Pacific Gas & Electric to shut down the electricity to millions of Californians for several days. Those without backup power (i.e., generators) were cut off. Those with electric vehicles were faced with the possibility that they might not be able to leave the affected areas.

Is Capitalism Inherently Unsustainable?

Capitalism is an economic model, one that allows people the opportunity to generate and retain one's own wealth. Around the world capitalism offers a development model that works at improving quality of life (measured by longevity, health, financial prosperity). We must face two sobering realities: first, we haven't figured out how to do that without sacrificing our planet (the environmental pillar) in the process, and secondly, that progress has not been universal or equitably distributed.

The idea of sustainability is based on a simple concept—that which can endure and last. Profits alone are not sustainable.

Simply put, when one compares the ecological footprint of countries with the human development index, it becomes obvious that we have a development path that successfully takes countries and people out of poverty, but it is at the expense of the planet. The lifestyles associated with development are massively resource consuming, using more resources than are available. Based on the resources on Earth, and the amount of consumption, the American lifestyle can be described as "five planet living," in Europe it is "three planet living" and in Saudi Arabia it is "six planet living."

This is not sustainable because we will eventually run out of resources to continue to enjoy these benefits.

When it comes to the social pillar, we face an even more daunting challenge. While we have generated a huge amount of financial wealth, the gap between the richest and the poorest of us has not gotten better, it has gotten worse. The rising tide is raising only some of the boats and the others are being left further behind. That is not just morally "unfair"; it also is politically and socially destabilizing. The Occupy movement and the powerful "We are the 99 percent" message have very effectively demonized "excessive wealth" as selfishness run amok and reflects growing frustration and resentment that can be a precursor to violent (France in 1789 and Russia in 1917) revolution. It can even lead to nonviolent revolution such as in 1989 when social, economic, and political forces in the German Democratic Republic (GDR; East Germany) led to the fall of the Berlin Wall and German reunification and the dissolution of the GDR. There is some evidence that the current civil war in Syria may have been caused (or made worse) by an environmental crisis (drought) in the southern portion of the country, when those facing starvation fled to the cities to seek jobs and relief (social) and the government was unable (or unwilling) to help (a failure of governance).[2]

It would be too easy, and rash, to simply blame "capitalism" for these ills. One need only look at the environmental impacts of other economic models. The GDR was widely known as the "most polluted nation" in Europe[3] (hardly an advertisement for socialism). The lower standards for the same quality of life indicators (longevity, health, and well-being) demonstrated the failings of Soviet Communism (once, of course, the truth became known).[4]

---

[2]JSTOR Daily. 2019. "Climate Change and Syria's Civil War." https://daily.jstor.org/climate-change-and-syrias-civil-war/, (accessed October 12, 2019).

[3]Christian Science Monitor. 1984. "East Germany Disputes Its Status as the Most Polluted Country in Europe." https://www.csmonitor.com/1984/1005/100538.html, (accessed October 12, 2019).

[4]Chicago Tribune. 1990. "Poverty, Hunger and Other Evils of Communism." https://www.chicagotribune.com/news/ct-xpm-1990-01-25-9001070410-story.html, (accessed October 12, 2019).

The concept of fiscal responsibility and responsible management is an integral element within any corporate sustainability program. From the boardrooms of Enron to the Deepwater Horizon crew members who recognized the dangers of continuing to drill but were ignored, no effort of corporate accountability can succeed without individuals accepting responsibility for their own actions and behaviors and being empowered to act on those values.

Business sustainability therefore will require buy-in by management as well as employees, based on the mutual understanding that when businesses that are respectful of the environment and universally advancing of the human condition are also profitable, it creates a virtuous cycle, one in which the benefits outweigh the costs of that business. Management must also understand the risks associated with short-term thinking as well as engaging in practices that they must keep hidden to remain successful.

Fortunately, as we shall explore further, these trends are converging at the same time.

Discussion Questions

1. The author cites examples of failures to illustrate the interdependence of environmental, social, and governance failures. Can you think of any examples where that balance has been successfully achieved?

2. Can you think of other examples when social or economic crises have led to political destabilization?

3. Is capitalism inherently unsustainable? Is it possible to take the "best" elements of capitalism, socialism and communism to define a "new" economic model? What would such a model look like?

CHAPTER 2

Integrating Sustainability into the Business

Introduction

For anyone, especially those in corporate leadership, to accept the premise that sustainability is a business strategy, we must demonstrate that it is a strategy that helps businesses meet their goals and enhance their reputations.

That businesses have responsibilities is not a new concept. They are responsible to provide their customers with safe products and services that meet their expectations and needs. They are responsible to pay their suppliers in a timely fashion. They are responsible for providing employees with, at a minimum, a safe workplace and a living wage (if not a career and self-actualization). They are responsible for conducting their businesses in a manner that adheres to the letter of the law. And, of course, businesses are responsible for providing those who invest in them with a return on their investment.

When it comes to sustainability, the language that is often used reflects a coalition of passionate and idealistic people within the organization. That is not enough. In fact, it can be detrimental if leadership sees your cadre as a band of well-meaning but naïve zealots trying to change the world rather than committed and dedicated business professionals who understand the business and what it takes to make it successful.

For this reason, it is important, always, to adopt and use the language of business rather than advocacy or philanthropy when integrating sustainability into any business. While most business disciplines have their own language, acronyms, and way of communicating, too often sustainability professionals speak in terms of "doing well by doing good" and the "Sustainable Development Goals" rather than the more compelling arguments that link sustainability programs to the established (and more familiar) business imperatives such as "improving business processes," "implementing best practices," and "return on investment."

In Lafarge S.A.'s 2003 Sustainability Report, Bertrand Collomb, chairman and CEO of Lafarge, who went on to head the World Business Council on Sustainable Development (WBCSD), described the "compelling case" for sustainability with words that were prescient:

> We are convinced that a global industrial group can only continue to be successful if it operates within the framework of sustainable development with a genuine concern for the environment. This commitment will help Lafarge to prepare for a future carbon-constrained world.

It is clear that, as a business leader, his primary concern was ensuring the long-term viability of the company. Knowing that the cement business is a major contributor to carbon dioxide emissions, he accepted the understanding that the need for emissions reductions would one day be a limiting factor if the company (and the entire industry) did not aggressively and proactively work to reduce them.

When you're talking about issues like safety, environmental stewardship, ethics, and fiscal responsibility, it is far more effective (it gains you more "reputational capital" and stakeholder goodwill) than to be very good at—and hanging your future on—doing what is required to avoid penalties.

Demonstrating that the future state is preferable to the existing is the secret to building a successful culture change, and corporate responsibility is no exception. Perhaps this is why corporate responsibility is gaining traction among the newest workers and those in business school today. And why those of us working in the space find ourselves increasingly answering the question "how" rather than "why."

Many critics of the corporate responsibility or sustainability model latch onto the famous maxim from American economist Milton Friedman (no relation):

> There is one and only one social responsibility of business—to use
> it resources and engage in activities designed to increase its profits

so long as it stays within the rules of the game, which is to say, engages in open and free competition without deception or fraud.[1]

This strict focus on the avoidance of legal misconduct is contradicted by his subsequent editorial in *The New York Times Magazine* on September 13, 1970 where he went on to acknowledge that the "rules of the game" also included societal expectations and norms:

> In a free-enterprise, private-property system, a corporate executive is an employee of the owners of the business. He has direct responsibility to his employers. That responsibility is to conduct the business in accordance with their desires, which generally will be to make as much money as possible while conforming to their basic rules of the society, both those embodied in law and those embodied in ethical custom.

Over the last three decades, history offers example after example of companies that obeyed the legal parameters but neglected the "rules of society ... embodied in ethical custom" and have ceased to be viable.

Anca Novacovici, LEED AP is the founder and president of Washington, DC-based Eco-Coach. For almost 15 years she has been working with organizations to implement sustainability, focusing on the business benefits.

> When I started out in 2006, I spent a lot of time educating businesses—and non-profits—about the benefits of going green, including the cost savings, acquiring new customer, growing sales, enhancing brand perceptions, attracting top talent and spurring innovation.

> Since then, the majority of the larger organizations, and increasingly medium-sized ones, have begun taking action and implementing environmentally sustainable practices with the understanding that it will benefit their business.[2]

---

[1]M. Friedman. 1962. *Capitalism and Freedom* (Chicago, IL: University of Chicago Press). https://www.press.uchicago.edu/ucp/books/book/chicago/C/bo18146821.html.
[2]A. Novacovici. September 23, 2019. Interview by the author.

One of the shifts Anca describes is the increasing awareness that environmental sustainability and going green is a "must have," not a "nice to have." This is being driven by to two things: the fact that sustainability makes business sense; and the increasing awareness and understanding of climate change and the impact that businesses have.

On August 19, 2019,[3] the Business Roundtable issued a "statement of corporate purpose" signed by the heads of more than 180 U.S. companies, including the CEOs of Amazon.com Inc, American Airlines (the largest airline in the world), and JPMorgan Chase & Co (America's largest bank) stating that businesses are responsible for providing economic benefits to all, not just its investors, and rejecting the notion of shareholder return being the primary purpose of a corporation. While they did acknowledge shareholders in the new statement, they focused on long-term shareholders and not the day-traders who often have no interest in the viability of the company but seek only a quick return on their investment.

This shows how society leads and defines the purpose of a business and introduces the first quantifiable business benefit of the sustainability model, the *social* license to operate.

Earning the Social License to Operate

It is an overused metaphor, but it is important to note that when the RMS Titanic sailed, the British Board of Trade required all vessels above 10,000 metric tons (11,023 U.S. tons) to carry 16 lifeboats. When Titanic was built, the regulations had not been updated for nearly 20 years. The Board stipulations were based on weight (rather than passenger numbers) and the vessel weighed more than four times the maximum the Board of Trade had considered. By carrying 16 lifeboats, the White Star line was exceeding the legal requirements by 25 percent (four boats), putting the Titanic, and the company, in an industry-leading position. As history teaches us, those regulations were revealed to be woefully inadequate on April 14, 1912, and two-thirds of the passengers and crew perished, even though

---

[3]A. Murray. 2019. "America's CEOs Seek a New Purpose for the Corporation," *Fortune*. https://fortune.com/longform/business-roundtable-ceos-corporations-purpose/, (accessed August 20, 2019).

more than half could have been saved because no one seriously considered the possibility of catastrophe until it was too late.

This is symptomatic of the fact that regulatory requirements are often deliberately responsive—put in place after a highly visible and catastrophic failure demonstrates the need for changes.

Companies that really want to be recognized as leaders (and gain the social license to operate from being ahead of expectations) need to make the strategic decision to take, and sometimes redefine, what it means to lead. Companies that are willing and ready to do this have rejected the notion that the failure to do things wrong is the same thing as doing things right.

People—including members of the community who the business hopes to attract as customers (and employees, suppliers, and the like) but also the regulatory agencies that are often necessary to grant permits—are not, and should not be, impressed by a company simply because it has not had any accidents, paid any penalties or because it has effective programs in place to rigorously and robustly meet the statutory requirements for its industry.

It does not qualify as leadership when an organization is satisfied at being among the best (or is the best) at meeting the minimum standards because relying on the failure or malfeasance of others in your space is not a valid business model. Conforming within acceptable legal limits will keep an organization out of court, but it will not "win" in the court of public opinion. Companies have come to understand that holding themselves accountable to a higher standard will keep them in good stead with their customers, employees, shareholders, suppliers, regulators and communities.

At a time when the industry standard was to measure the accident rate by using hours worked by full-time employees, Lafarge made the decision to include contractors and subcontractors. "Lafarge's objective is to reach zero incidents over the long-term and across all the units, with contractors working to the same standards as employees," stated a company publication. "Moreover, Lafarge wants to be recognized by NGOs and the business community as a world leader in safety."[4] The company

---

[4]Lafarge. 2011. "Sustainability Report." https://www.lafargeholcim.com/archives/05182012-publication_sustainable_development-Sustainable_report_2011-health-safety-uk.pdf, (accessed August 9, 2019).

recognized that, in addition to putting itself at a morally leading position, taking such an action would send a ripple through the construction materials industry, which had a direct positive impact on the company's reputation for being committed to safety beyond its own employees. Doing this was a brave stance because initially it meant reporting a *higher incident rate* than its competitors, but by publicly announcing and reporting against the higher intention, suddenly the dialogue changed from a group of competitors each promoting their accomplishments to who was setting the standard by which everyone was to be compared and measured. "If they adopt our standards, that means they're admitting we're the leader," explained one senior executive.

The hard part for many companies is determining what the new rules of the game are. For international companies this is even more complicated because both laws and social customs vary widely.

Dr. Wayne Visser, professor of Integrated Value and holder of the Chair in Sustainable Transformation at Antwerp Management School, explains:

> Organizations are embedded parts in a larger global socio-ecological system. And one of the reasons why organizations go into decline or fail is that they do not have sufficient understanding of the complex, changing patterns that make up their operating context.
>
> For example, organizations may underestimate the significance of gradual shifts in societal norms, or they may be unprepared for dramatic disruptive crises. They may fail to see how changes in their complex value chains or public policy frameworks are having ripple effects across their competitive landscape.[5]

On the day that Canadian Prime Minister Justin Trudeau was sworn in, he announced that his cabinet would be 50 percent men and 50 percent women. When asked why this was important to him, Trudeau received international attention for responding: "Because it is 2015." Some of the

---

[5] W. Visser. 2019. "Integrated Value Management: Implementing Sustainable Transformation," *AMS Sustainable Transformation Briefing Series*, no. 5. Antwerp Management School. http://www.waynevisser.com/articles.

attention lauded him for being progressive, some pointed out that this was just catching up with demographics, and still others found it appalling that women would be placed in high positions in government. Your own reaction to that last sentence will be based on many things, including the cultural norms that have formed your attitudes and opinions.

Similarly, the principle of equal pay for equal work is not a universal standard. It is codified in the legislation of the 28 countries within the European Union, Iceland, Liechtenstein, and Norway. Macedonia and Turkey, which hope to join the EU, have passed legislation to match the EU standards (Figure 2.1).

The concept of "The Butterfly Effect" explains that even small actions can have far-reaching and unintended consequences. This presents a unique problem for businesses operating in a global context because any business working across cultures must face the fact that, no matter how they conduct their business, they are going to have some impacts that will cause some stakeholders to question their actions and—often more seriously—their intentions.

Organizations like the Global Reporting Initiative, the United Nations, the Organisation for Economic Co-operation and Development (OECD), and others have attempted to define minimum sets of standards for global business. But, as we have seen, conforming to any standards (even global guidelines) is not a leadership position.

Fundamentally, the question comes down to two extremes—whether people see businesses as having a responsibility to follow the "highest" (often equated by one's own) standards and to serve as a driver for changes (seen as improvements) or whether they believe that the businesses have a responsibility to be respectful and protective of the local indigenous cultures wherever they do business.

While these two extremes exaggerate the point, the question is fundamental for a business that must consider which most closely reflects the attitudes and opinions of their stakeholders (including shareholder and customers) back home. And it is important to note at the outset that some cultural differences do not require crossing international boundaries; standards and values also can and do vary within nations.

The issue is lessened in cases when (and where) the local culture is one that does not conflict severely with that of stakeholders in the

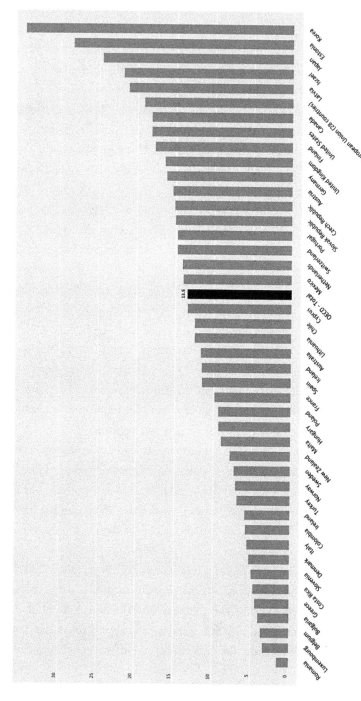

Figure 2.1 The gender wage gap is defined as the difference between median earnings of men and women relative to median earnings of men.

Source: OECD, 2019, Gender wage gap (indicator).*

*OECD. 2019. "Gender Wage Gap (Indicator)." https://data.oecd.org/earnwage/gender-wage-gap.htm, (accessed August 9, 2019).

organization's home country. A business operating in a culture with different perspectives on what constitutes appropriate wages, benefits, working conditions, hours, and age of employment may find itself struggling to explain its practices both back home *and* in its host countries.

Today we look back at the age of colonization with the perspective of history and are critical of efforts to "rescue" people from their traditional religious beliefs. We see those civilizations and societies as being worthy of protection rather than extermination. But at that time, the Spanish conquistadors saw themselves as liberators rather than as oppressors. Their "modern" sensibilities were appalled by human sacrifices and other tenets of the Maya religion and sought to help by bringing local populations the benefits of their more "advanced" thinking. In other words, they thought that they were doing the right and moral thing.

In his book *Moral Capitalism* Steven Young, global executive director of the Caux Round Table, stresses the critical importance of being mindful and respectful of the local indigenous cultures that may be ill-equipped to "fight back" against a more technologically advanced one.

> The culture that follows upon successful economic growth is a global one, rooted in American consumerism ... that subverts traditional elites and values. Global business is the carrier of this culture, responding to consumer demands. It is legitimate for business to deliver what people want, but at the same time business should take care that local cultures are not permanently asphyxiated.[6]

It is important to note that "American consumerism"—which has been the dominant (most successful) model in the 20th century—is a relatively recent phenomenon for both America and human history. It is not, as some have suggested, a "core value." When we return to America's foundational documents, we find that many of the principles and values that the nation's founders held dear support the mind-set of sustainability and long-term thinking.

---

[6]S. Young. 2003. *Moral Capitalism* (San Francisco, CA: Berrett-Koehler Publishers, pp. 175–6). https://www.penguinrandomhouse.com/books/574689/moral-capitalism-by-stephen-young/.

Those who made their primary living off the land—like George Washington, Thomas Jefferson, and many others, understood and respected the importance of caring for the environment. George Washington took pains to plant native trees—some of which still live today—on his Mount Vernon estate. Despite the seemingly endless munificence of the new continent, he also experimented with the use of living hedges, or dense thorny shrubs, to keep animals from destroying plants, to conserve timber.

For the social pillar one need look no further than both of America's most fundamental foundational documents—the Declaration of Independence and the Constitution—to reflect an understanding of the power of diversity and including multiple perspectives. The Declaration is headed "In Congress...," which does not refer to the legislative body (which did not exist at that time) but rather meaning that the document reflected the combined wisdom, passion, ideas, and perspectives of a group of people. The Constitution begins with the powerful phrase "We the people...," deriving its basis from the combined will of the people within the country. Thomas Jefferson, in his writings about the role of representative government, stated:

> All, too, will bear in mind this sacred principle, that though the will of the majority is in all cases to prevail, that will to be rightful must be reasonable; that the minority possess their equal rights, which equal law must protect, and to violate would be oppression.[7]

The founders recognized, as progressive companies have, that bringing to bear a wealth of opinions and differing perspectives is the key to competitive advantage.

As for long-term versus short-term thinking, after the United States earned its independence, the founders again convened to draft its Constitution. This document makes it clear that the purpose of the nation was not only for the benefit of its current citizens. Indeed, the preamble states that the purpose of the document is to "secure the blessings

---

[7] T. Jefferson. 1801. "First Inaugural Address." https://www.history.org/Almanack/people/jeffinaug1.cfm, (accessed October 12, 2019).

of liberty to ourselves and our posterity, do ordain and establish this Constitution for the United States of America." It remains the seminal foundational document for the nation. When the president takes the oath of office, he (or she) swears to preserve, protect, and defend it.

Today people expect businesses to bring their benefits (goods, services, jobs) while working within the local culture. In fact, being respectful of those cultural differences is sometimes a requirement placed upon the company prior to being allowed to do business.

Because businesses often bring with them the culture of their home country, cultural norms are often a secondary, unexpected impact on a new community. Those impacts can range from the mundane (different foods, music, styles of dress—although that can be disruptive as well) to the dramatic, such as providing salaries (and the empowerment having one's own money brings) to individuals who have previously been excluded from the economic mainstream. A business executive from the United States received gasps while leading a business meeting in Morocco when he unintentionally challenged the prevailing local culture by asking a woman for her opinion in a business meeting.

Young recognizes that however well intended, the very existence of a business from another culture threatens the local social, political, religious, and political orders and challenges the status quo. Therefore, he writes, "business has a responsibility to moderate its impact on those communities, which can hardly protect themselves against the intrusions."

There are other rules that businesses must adhere to if they wish to be successful, such as the obvious rules of the marketplace including supply and demand. But the fundamental principle of social license to operate is that the communities where a company wishes to do business need to "buy-in" before the company has a chance to sell them anything.

Socrates said that "the way to gain a good reputation is to endeavor to be what you desire to appear."[8] It is important to note that he acknowledges that people attribute values based on acting in accordance with aspirations. In other words, people judge based on the impact of both

[8]https://www.goodreads.com/quotes/8604656-the-way-to-gain-a-good-reputation-is-to-endeavor, (accessed August 9, 2019).

actions and intentions. It is unlikely that anyone (individual or company) can truly achieve perfection.

The lessons for corporations are clearly transferable. A company that is viewed as a positive and favorable member of the community is likely to have less opposition, and when—as is almost inevitable—a misstep does occur, it is more likely to be viewed as an aberration rather than symptomatic of a greater and negative truth. Like any other business expense, a clear case can be made that investing time, money, and resources to build "reputational capital" is a valid business effort to ensure success over the long term.

Ultimately the role of business in a global society will be determined by the global society. Achieving consensus will remain elusive, but in the end, people (and not businesses) will decide whether transgressions are severe enough to require legislation or whether businesses will stay within the parameters that social convention dictates. The Business Roundtable statement either represents an attempt to avoid that regulation or a true reflection, and acknowledgment, of the fact that society has already changed the rules of the game.

Discussion Questions

1. How can a business be both respectful of indigenous cultures and promote a "higher" standard?

2. Who decides what those values are?

3. Can and how would a business justify actions to its stakeholders who may find those practices to be questionable?

4. The American model of capitalism was dominant in the 20th century. Which model/models do you think will dominate in the 21st century? Which should?

5. Do you believe that business leaders have acknowledged a change in the role of business in society or are they simply "saying the right thing" and committed to "business as usual?" What evidence can you find to support your opinion? What evidence (actions) would be necessary to change your mind?

Reducing or Avoiding Costs

In business, the adage "time is money" takes on new urgency. Every delay, whether it be in permitting, construction, recruiting or training employees, or opening for business, has an associated cost in lost revenue, due to the combination of costs of capital (interests on loans, salaries, utility costs, etc.) and loss of revenue and opportunity when another company can use any time advantage to establish itself in the market, cherry-pick the local talent pool, and build relationships with customers and suppliers.

Each day that a store remains vacant or a commercial lot lies undeveloped is a day of lost sales revenue for the company. The community does not realize the benefits of having those goods or services available, workers are denied employment, and the community cannot collect sales and income taxes.

A company that has a positive reputation has a competitive advantage. While communities may not actively facilitate approval of a permit, myriad of examples exist where community opposition has resulted in substantial delays, requiring a greater investment of time and money.

This is a lesson that is sometimes more clearly demonstrated by its failure. "We recognize that we need a 'license' to operate in any community that we enter," wrote David Weidman, president and CEO of Celanse Corp. in *NYSE Magazine*'s August/September 2006 issue. "Some of those licenses have been lost because of social irresponsibility on the part of some companies within our industry. So, this license to operate demands that we be actively involved in the community."

Most businesses know the importance of investing in preventive maintenance to keep equipment in good working order. In fact, these "expenses" are not considered optional. Those who do not invest in this manner are considered foolish and viewed with contempt. But there are other, direct ways that businesses can save money through a longer-term approach such as investing in high-efficiency equipment that saves energy and/or reduces the amount of waste generated, and the like.

Gaining Market Opportunity or Advantage

Whether you define it as enhanced goodwill or reduced opposition, sustainability programs that position the company as a positive corporate citizen can impact the speed with which the company enters or grows within a market (the social license to operate). But what opportunities exist for environmentally or socially responsible *products and services?*

Customers want, deserve, and increasingly demand a superior customer experience, however they (the customers) define it. Southwest Airlines has raised this to a new standard, offering a clear demonstration that low-cost and first-class service are not at the opposite ends of the continuum. Southwest Airlines flight attendants are known for customizing the routine safety announcements, adding humor and personality to what is an important (but often lackluster) task. The result is not only increased passenger engagement in information that can save their lives, but also a visible demonstration of a company culture that values diversity and inclusion.

Making a clear claim to sustainable attributes requires clarity of message. A plastic bottle that says "30 percent less plastic" is much less credible than "made from 100 percent recycled plastic" not only because the number is lower, but because it does not give a clear indication of how much plastic has been reduced. And while consumers may not fully understand labels such as "organic," "fair trade certified," or even "EnergyStar," those terms do drive customer preference. That is why it is important to "send the visual cues" so that customers can be attracted not only to the attributes but also the value that they place on having others recognize those attributes.

Does it work? According to the Fairtrade International 2017 to 2018 Annual Report, global sales of Fairtrade products rose by 8 percent to nearly $9.2 billion in 2017, generating Fairtrade Premiums of more than $193 million for farmers' and workers' organizations. The United States now ranks as the third largest market for Fairtrade goods behind the United Kingdom and Germany. Retail sales in the United States topped $1 billion.

From 2016 to 2017 the volume of Fairtrade coffee sold grew by 15 percent, reaching 214,106 metric tons. The fastest growing markets for Fairtrade coffee included Ireland, Finland, and Denmark, with growth rates of 36 percent, 35 percent, and 25 percent, respectively.

In the United States, Fairtrade cocoa sales increased 33 percent. Bananas and avocados earned 51 percent and 58 percent growth, apiece. Fairtrade coffee farmers benefited from a 24.5 percent sales increase.

In 2018 Unilever announced[9] its "Sustainable Living" brands grew 46 percent faster than the rest of the business and delivered 70 percent of its turnover growth. It also explained that their portfolio of sustainable brands has outperformed the average rate of growth at Unilever for the last 4 years.

This kind of market growth is something that most companies can only aspire to achieve. Sustainability claims clearly can be a differentiator, as long as they are credible and tie into issues that motivate people.

Discussion Questions

1. Some people believe that doing good should be its own reward and that earning a premium for doing so somehow sullies the effort. What do you think?

2. How much of a price premium should people pay for "sustainable" (responsible) goods?

3. Is there an argument to be made that less responsible products (i.e., those that contribute to climate change, use new rather than recycled materials) should cost more?

4. How would one begin going about calculating and charging for those costs?

---

[9]Press Release. October 5, 2018. "Unilever's Sustainable Living Plan Continues to Fuel Growth." https://www.unilever.com/news/press-releases/2018/unilevers-sustainable-living-plan-continues-to-fuel-growth.html, (accessed August 9, 2019).

Maximizing and Leveraging Employee Engagement

Brands are intangible assets, created by the emotions that people feel when they experience, purchase, or use your products; interact with your employees; see your name on the side of a vehicle on the road; and a myriad of other uncontrolled interactions that happen throughout their lifetime.

This is why one of the most essential, but sadly often overlooked or taken for granted, stakeholder groups is a company's employees. Beyond the "feel good" aspect that is often cited as one of the softer (less business focused) benefits of sustainability, employee morale and culture are linked to productivity, recruitment, and retention.

While many companies talk about how their employees are their most valuable assets, those that consider employees as integral partners in the organization's future and success recognize the power of true employee engagement. Employees who are passionate about the company and its products are the best advocates and can counteract threats to brand image simply by talking to their neighbors and friends outside the work setting, in addition to serving as ambassadors for your brand when they interact with members of the public when acting in their official capacity.

Earlier we highlighted the Southwest Airlines' safety announcement as part of an improved customer experience. At the same time, can there be a better recruitment tool than passenger videos on social media showing those announcements? Some have reached millions of impressions—without spending a single marketing dollar.

Any failure to engage employees results in behavior that can damage profitability directly. Poor morale can lead to passive sabotage in the form of reduced productivity, shoddy workmanship and quality control, and increased absenteeism. At its worst, unhappy employees can and do engage in behavior that deliberately hurts the company, such as an employee who shares information about a corporate problem. This can result in damage to corporate image, credibility, and the bottom line ranging from lost sales to increased costs due to fines and penalties.

No matter how well the press release is written, how many millions of dollars are spent on advertising, the image of any company or organization is in the hands of the company or organization's employees; and the image is managed by the actions, behaviors, and attitudes of those employees. Good PR or marketing cannot overcome a bad reality. The everyday actions of employees—how they treat customers and represent your brand by their actions—influence the way that customers feel about the company. A good reality is the best way to build a positive brand; employees are therefore integral.

A single employee steered the Exxon Valdez into Bligh Reef in Prince William Sound and had more control over Exxon's brand than the combined talents of their corporate communications department, public relations, and marketing agencies and teams combined. Similarly, when Captain Sullenberger successfully glided his crippled airliner into the Hudson River, he also had U.S. Airways' reputation in his hands as well as the lives of his passengers. While the corporate "brand police" might have cringed over how prominent the logo was on the side of the jet, they can take no credit for how the reputation of the company was enhanced by Sully's actions that day.

FedEx, a company that prides itself on reliability and being on time used social media to respond to a news photo showing one of their truck drivers helping to save the life of another driver who was caught in a flash flood. Their response explaining that sometimes it was worth being a little late (along with the photo) reinforced their brand values and also humanized the company.

Fear of the negative sometimes prevents companies from taking advantage of the huge upside potential of empowering their workforce as brand ambassadors. After all, who knows a company better than its employees? If that is not something a business is proud to share, its problems will not be solved by keeping employees in the dark and hoping that they stay quiet. They're telling someone.

A failure to consider employees as vital in the organization's overall success can compromise a company's competitive position. One company discovered that employees who had not been informed of the corporate strategy to prevent competitors from entering the local market by making a show of maintaining a visible presence through the highly active upkeep of a nonworking production facility (including painting, landscaping, and the like) unwittingly compromised the effort by publicly complaining about the "stupid" manager forcing them to do so. This unintentional sabotage of the company strategy demonstrates the importance of engaging employees in the strategy and the power that they have to impact the success—or failure—of its efforts.

The most fundamental reason for empowering employees and engaging them in sustainability programs is the same reason local employees are the best at dealing with customers, communities, regulators, etc.

Empowering employees is also critical because they can help define how the program is implemented by identifying local issues, opinion leaders, and opportunities. But an even more valuable role is that they are closest to, and therefore able to identify, the impediments whether they be cultural, religious, or rooted in the existing official and unofficial power structures. If a company wants to win the battle for hearts and minds, they will do it by actively engaging their employees and treating them as the heart of their success.

This, of course, supposes that workers are already attracted to your business. According to a PwC report "Millennials at Work—Reshaping the workplace," corporate social values become more important to millennials when choosing an employer once their basic needs, like adequate pay and working conditions, are met. The report states that "millennials want their work to have a purpose, to contribute something to the world and they want to be proud of their employer."[10]

Discussion Questions

1. Would you accept a lower salary to work for an organization that more closely aligns with your values?

2. How would your financial obligations (debts, loans, responsibility for more than just yourself) factor into that decision?

---

[10]PWC. 2011. "Millennials at Work." https://www.pwc.de/de/prozessoptimierung/ assets/millennials-at-work-2011.pdf, (accessed August 9, 2019).

Seizing the Innovation High Ground

Companies that are looking for ways to be more environmentally, socially, and economically responsible are driving innovations in products, services, and sourcing as well as financial acumen. While they may sometimes struggle to find a market, success can be transformational. LED light bulbs were initially very expensive and a niche product. Today's bulbs not only provide the same light spectrum as classic incandescent bulbs, they use 75 or 80 percent less electricity to do so—paying for themselves in about half a year in energy savings. In 2006, Wal-Mart, the world's largest retailer, announced plans to sell one bulb to each of its 100 million customers. Not only does the planet benefit from the reduction in energy use, but companies like General Electric that produce the bulbs also benefit from increased sales (and reputation). Companies that are seen as innovative tend to attract innovative employees, and the cycle accelerates. That is good for business.

Similar success can be found in the example of electric vehicles. The General Motors EV1 was an electric car produced and leased by General Motors from 1996 to 1999. While customer reaction to the EV1 was positive, GM believed that electric cars occupied an unprofitable niche of the automobile market and ended up crushing most of the cars. By 2012, when Tesla released the Model S, both the vehicle and the market were ready. The Model S earned high praise from automotive enthusiasts, earned the highest safety rating of all time from Consumer Reports, and was the top selling electric vehicle in both 2015 and 2016, displaced by the lower-priced Nissan Leaf. Today car manufacturers from Audi to Volkswagen offer a range of electric vehicles. This includes BMW, Chevrolet, Honda, , Hyundai, Kia, and Toyota. In the top three markets, the United States, China, and Europe combined, more than 5,000,000 light duty electric vehicles are on the road. That remains a small percentage of the total, but the growth trend is undeniable (and unstoppable).

Sir Richard Branson founded the Carbon War Room[11] because he saw not only the threat of climate change but also the opportunities created

---

[11]https://www.virgin.com/richard-branson/story-carbon-war-room.

by the threat. An article for Huffington Post (written by this author) bears quoting at some length:

> "I have described the increasing levels of greenhouse gases in the atmosphere as one of the greatest threats to the ongoing prosperity and sustainability of life on the planet," (Branson) says. "The good news is that creating businesses that will power our growth and reduce our carbon output while protecting resources is also the greatest wealth-generating opportunity of our generation."

History seems to bear witness to his perspective. A high percentage of the wealthiest people in history—excluding despots and conquerors—have made their fortunes in the areas of energy, transportation, and construction. The Rockefeller fortune was based on oil (energy), Andrew Carnegie (steel), and Cornelius Vanderbilt saw the revolution from wind to steam engines and built an empire in shipping and railroads. Henry Ford ushered in the basis for decades of industry as he took the automobile from the purview of the wealthy to a staple of the average American with the introduction of the assembly line. By increasing production efficiency thereby reducing costs for consumers and creating an entire industry much as Bill Gates did for the personal computer. Andrew William Mellon went from banking to construction, energy, and transportation (lumber, oil, steel, shipbuilding, and construction).

Many of the changes in industry and transportation have followed the evolution from individual power (feet or paddles), to animal power (horses and horses and buggies) to steam (initially powered in the U.S. by wood and then coal) and finally to internal combustion and electricity. It is important to note that in addition to increasing speed and efficiency, many of these changes were furthered by the desire for more environmentally friendly alternatives; streetcars and buses in New York were seen as a solution to the manure that was lining the city streets. The progression for shipping (in the cases of our military submarines) has progressed on to nuclear power.

Electricity is generated by a combination of means, including hydroelectric, wind, solar, nuclear, and coal-fired power plants. In Germany, government subsidies and programs have helped support the expansion of solar and other efforts. The recent decision to eliminate nuclear from that nation's portfolio is an interesting experiment in progress. In the U.S., the vast majority of our power is generated by coal-fired plants. These plants are a lot cleaner than in past decades, and mining techniques have improved, but this remains an environmentally intensive way to power our myriad of electronic devices. (Author's Note: This is no longer accurate. Since this article was originally published in 2012, U.S. power generation has shifted toward natural gas and renewables. Natural gas surpassed coal in 2015. In 2019 renewables generated more electricity than coal.)

If fortunes are to be made by the bold who seize the innovation high ground (and those who invest in those individuals and technologies) then the needs to address climate change, energy independence, and meet the needs of a population that has reached seven billion worldwide combine to demand action to build a sustainable world economy.

So where are the greatest opportunities? If we look at the traditional sectors—energy, construction, and transportation—one of the biggest things that leaps out is the idea of substituting and replacing raw materials using one thing that humans seem to be able to produce in abundance—waste.

The Environmental Protection Agency (EPA) estimates that more than 50 percent of global methane emissions are related to human-related activities such as fossil fuel production, animal husbandry, food production, biomass burning, and waste management. These activities release significant quantities of methane to the atmosphere. Tapping these sources is a win–win because it prevents greenhouse gas emissions and can provide fuel for power plants to generate electricity.

Synthetic gypsum has been used to make wallboard in the United States for more than 20 years. Electric power plants that burn coal are required to have scrubbers that trap emissions. The result is a very pure synthetic gypsum that is being used to create wallboard. Since 2000, enough gypsum to finish the interiors of more than 7 million American homes has come from this waste product. Similarly, wastewater treatment produces biomethane, which can be captured, cleaned, and injected into the natural gas pipeline system. By preventing methane from escaping into the atmosphere and burning it for heat (or to generate electricity), this renewable fuel source emits far fewer greenhouse gas emissions.[12]

A word of caution is warranted here. Colin Stackhouse, an executive with Siemens for almost 20 years, worries that companies and investors may be tempted to focus their efforts instead on the short-term opportunities that come from mitigating the impacts of climate change:

> When it comes to risk, companies need to factor in adaptation, because the impacts of climate change are already here—effecting everything from supply chains to operations as well as basic needs like air conditioning. Unfortunately, it is likely that the short-term profits to be gained by preventing the worst impacts of climate change may lead those of mitigation efforts because the local and immediate needs will be undeniable ... and the quickest money will be in solving the problems, not preventing them.[13]

In 2013 Collomb wrote in *Global Agenda Magazine* that he believed that European-based companies might have "a natural advantage" based on that continent's more socially conscious culture. He conceded, on the other hand, that the cultural advantages of bold innovation, responsiveness to changing market conditions and expectations, and an entrepreneurial spirit might give the advantage to American companies.

The question of who will seize the innovation high ground is precisely what is now being asked thanks to the Business Roundtable's updated Statement of Purpose.

---

[12]J. Friedman. 2012. "Climate Change: Good for Business." https://www.huffpost.com/entry/the-best-news-about-clima_b_1274873, (accessed August 9, 2019).
[13]C. Stackhouse. July 18, 2019. Interview by the author.

Discussion Questions

1. Will the "easy money" that comes from mitigating climate change (i.e., the opportunity to sell more climate control systems) reduce the imperative to address climate change?
2. How do we prevent that from happening?
3. Is there a social inequity issue in the fact that those who contribute least to climate change are likely to bear the brunt of its impacts?
4. Which cultural overlay for capitalism (American, European, Asian, Other, a mixture) will define capitalism in the 21st century? Which should?

Attracting Investment Capital

One of the trends in investing in the wake of the 2008 global financial crisis is how investors have gravitated to socially responsible investment (SRI) funds and companies that have earned reputation for strong ethical leadership. Investments have swelled from $3.07 to $12 trillion between 2012 and 2017.[14] Several factors may contribute to this, including the fact that the SRI portfolio performed better and recovered its value quicker in post crisis than the non-SRI portfolio, indicating that SRI portfolios are more resilient to economic turmoil and market shocks (Figure 2.2).[15]

Today one out of every four dollars under professional management in the United States is involved in socially responsible investing. It is worth pointing out that the financial mess, as well as the vast majority of market crashes following economic "bubbles" came from people and organizations chasing the "fast buck" and not concentrating on sustainable growth.

That represents a huge—and growing—pool of money that is being invested in companies that have been found to be sustainable. And because

[14]Forum for Sustainable and Responsible Investment. https://www.ussif.org/sribasics, (accessed August 9, 2019).
[15]J. Wu, G. Lodorfos, A. Dean, and G. Gioulmpaxiotisb. 2015. "The Market Performance of Socially Responsible Investment During Periods of the Economic Cycle - Illustrated Using the Case of FTSE. Managerial and Decision Economics." https://doi.org/10.1002/mde.2772, (accessed August 9, 2019).

Investors using socially responsible criteria hit $12 trillion in U.S. assets

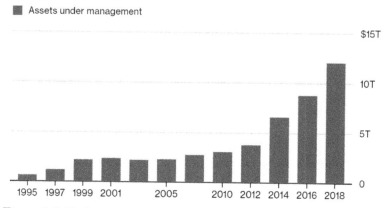

Figure 2.2 Today a quarter of the money under professional management in the United States is invested in socially responsible investing, up from one out of every eight dollars in 2012.

Source: US SIF.

these funds are dedicated to both short-term and long-term growth (rather than day trading or quarterly results) the investors are "stakeholders" in long-term results of the businesses that they are supporting.

At the same time, because of the profile of SRI investors, businesses can be confident in this investment pool. The primary sources of SRI investment come from:

- Individuals who invest part of their savings or retirement plans in mutual funds that specialize in seeking companies with good labor and environmental practices;
- Credit unions and community development banks that have a specific mission of serving low- and middle-income communities;
- Hospitals and medical schools that refuse to invest in tobacco companies;
- Foundations that support community development loan funds and other high social impact investments in line with their missions;
- Religious institutions that file shareholder resolutions to urge companies in their portfolios to meet strong ethical and governance standards;

- Venture capitalists that identify and develop companies that produce environmental services, create jobs in low-income communities, or provide other societal benefits;
- Responsible property funds that help develop or retrofit residential and commercial buildings to high-energy efficiency standards;
- Public pension plan officials who have encouraged companies in which they invest to reduce their greenhouse gas emissions and to factor climate change into their strategic planning.

Sustainable investing has continued to grow, with 85 percent of U.S. individual investors expressing interest in sustainable investing strategies, according to a 2019 study from Morgan Stanley.[16]

Being recognized as a sustainable business provides access to this investment capital that is specifically seeking to make investments in businesses that are well run and prepared to do business over the long term.

According to research by Monks and Lajoux, authors of *Corporate Valuation for Portfolio Investment: Analyzing Assets, Earnings, Cash Flow, Stock Price, Governance, and Special Situations*[17] fully 80 percent of the market value of Standard and Poor's 500 companies comes from intangible assets. In 2005, Apple's market value was $58 billion. The total tangible assets on its balance sheet made up less than one-fifth (19.8 percent) of that value. More than 80 percent of the company's value was contained in its relationships with its stakeholders.

Each stakeholder relationship is an intangible asset of the business. As any accountant can explain, assets can appreciate, depreciate, or hold their value. Effectively managing these relationships increases the opportunities and lowers the risk contained within each relationship. So, by

[16]A. Brown. 2019. "Sustainable Investing At All-Time High, Says Morgan Stanley," *Triple Pundit.* https://www.triplepundit.com/story/2019/sustainable-investing-all-time-high-says-morgan-stanley/84916/?fbclid=IwAR1Vc6z-xxEHT2M6-VZ_gyjgo0gV27oOSMHXTQu2k4M3noGm3jXeNw1K8xc, (accessed September 17, 2019).

[17]R. Monks and A.R. Lajoux. 2010. *Corporate Valuation for Portfolio Investment: Analyzing Assets, Earnings, Cash Flow, Stock Price, Governance, and Special Situations* (Hoboken, NJ: Bloomberg Press). https://www.amazon.com/Corporate-Valuation-Portfolio-Investment-Governance/dp/1576603172, (accessed November 9, 2010).

enhancing the quality of its stakeholder relationships a company increases its intangible assets and the overall valuation of the business.

Therefore, the salient question becomes, how to effectively manage your relationships with customers, employees, owners/investors, suppliers, competitors, communities, and government agencies and regulators?

For each group the principles of integrity, authenticity, and engagement—engaging in open dialogue rather than treating them as audiences who receive information—apply.

Another financial benefit to a sustainable corporation is the focus on governance and ethics. Well-managed companies present less risk. Corporate reputation, governance, and ethics are headline issues associated with corporate social responsibility including the ethics of arms and defense deals, "fat cat" salaries and shareholder activism, illegal workers and supply chain issues, the financial scandals and the infamous collapses of Enron and WorldCom, and false accounting. Companies that are seen to manage their risks better are seen as wiser investments.

The other side of this equation (the stick as opposed to the carrot) is that as the risks of climate change have become more pronounced, so have efforts by major investment firms to push companies to be more sustainable. Bloomberg reported that, while the preference of institutional investors is still to engage—through conversations and shareholder resolutions—some investment houses like Legal & General Investment Management (LGIM) have gone to more extreme measures—divestment. Bloomberg reported on August 7, 2019 that LGIM had sold about $300 million worth of its Exxon shares and would use its remaining stake to vote against the reappointment of Chairman and Chief Executive Officer Darren Woods.

The article went on to explain that Mark Lewis, who leads climate change investment research for BNP Paribas Asset Management, compares these actions to the efforts that forced companies to divest from in apartheid-era South Africa in the mid-1980s, helping end that government's official policy of racial segregation and discrimination. In March, BNP Paribas announced that its actively managed funds would exit almost $1.1 billion of coal stocks as early as next year. The news was met with some outrage, but Lewis defended the decision based on long-range economics rather than short-term possible returns.

A few years ago, investors would have jumped onto the prospect of owning shares in the Saudi Arabian Oil Company (the world's largest oil and gas company by revenue) but the IPO has hit several stumbling blocks—including achieving an acceptable valuation. While the company is immensely profitable, concerns about environmental, social, and governance (ESG) issues (including human rights, the murder of *Washington Post* columnist Jamal Khashoggi, and challenges from at least some investors who are choosing to avoid fossil fuel investments in favor of investments deemed more environmentally friendly) have hampered the effort to bring the company public. Companies like Singapore's Temasek Holdings decided against investing in the IPO. Aramco also received a lukewarm response from the Abu Dhabi Investment Authority. At the same time, to be fair, other investment groups including Barclays Plc, BNP Paribas SA, Deutsche Bank AG and UBS Group AG, Credit Agricole SA, Gulf International Bank BSC, and Societe Generale SA have signed on. This raises an important issue: is the best way to encourage businesses to be more transparent and responsible to hold out a lofty standard, or welcome those who at least seem to express a desire to be sustainable and help them evolve?

There are some companies and industries that people love to hate. Critics of the sustainability and socially responsible investing are very quick to point out the high rates of returns for the so-called "sin" companies: those that produce products like cigarettes (a favorite example) and continue to thrive despite overwhelming evidence that their products are unhealthy for people and the planet.

But there is a vast gray area. Companies that produce bottled water are criticized for the production and packaging of life-sustaining commodity that, people argue, needlessly wastes resources. Certainly, those in the developed world would do well to drink from their tap using reusable containers but we cannot forget that the demand for water has outpaced population growth, 785 million people do not have access to drinking water services and half the world's population is already experiencing severe water scarcity at least 1 month a year according to the United Nations.[18] At least one in four people is likely to live in a country affected

---

[18]Sustainable Development Goals. 2019. "Water and Sanitation." https://www .un.org/sustainabledevelopment/water-and-sanitation/, (accessed October 12, 2019).

by chronic or recurring shortages of fresh water. Those bottled water companies may be the best way to provide these people with life-giving water free from bacteria, parasites, and animal (including human) waste. As the problems with the public water supply in Flint, Michigan, or after natural disasters demonstrate, those products are essential when the infrastructure breaks down.

Fast food companies are criticized for everything from the lack of nutritional value of their products to their packaging, their marketing to young people, and their predominance in lower-income neighborhoods. While certainly their products can be linked to obesity, it is important to remember that the World Health Organization estimates that one-third of the world is underfed and one-third is starving. In Haiti, where cookies made of dirt, salt, and vegetable shortening have become a regular staple, the same McDonald's hamburger nutritionists scoff at would be a blessing.

Gun manufacturers who produce weapons that take away thousands of innocent lives also allow hunters to provide sustenance for their families—often more humanely than more primitive hunting methods that cause the animals pain and suffering or even leave them injured and susceptible to disease. While we indulge ourselves in guilt for being on the top of the food chain, an estimated 6 million people will starve to death this year alone.

Another example is a company that pledged greenhouse gas emissions reduction targets and demonstrated that it was working toward them in a manner that was consistent with the Paris Agreement and the "well below 2 degrees" target found itself being singled out for criticism by those who did not know, understand, or were unwilling to accept that the company was doing its part, based on the same science those activists were citing as their reason for protesting.

These examples are meant to be extreme, but they lead to an important question. Should we continue to shun companies that engage in (some) activities that we don't like even as they make real progress such as improving their packaging and distribution? Or instead should we offer the olive branch of positive reinforcement even as we hope that these are merely preliminary efforts toward a more enlightened approach to providing value?

And is it fundamentally much different than the Bill and Melinda Gates Foundation's efforts (which are often praised) to fight diseases? Recall that the foundation owes its existence to the sales of computers that are made of petroleum-based plastics and precious metals that are often mined, created, and disposed of in ways that are detrimental to health and the environment.

Sales of "unhealthy" choices are unaffected when we insist that food companies share the nutritional content of their products. Warning labels on cigarettes explicitly detail the dangers and yet do not prevent countless of intelligent human beings—a disproportionate number of whom can ill afford the expense of the cigarettes, much less the medical care that often comes from smoking—from taking up the habit each year. Are we holding the companies unfairly accountable for providing goods and services that the market demands?

The SRI community must reward and recognize achievements as we move toward a sustainable global economy; remembering that improvements along the path are worthy of recognition because it is the best way to encourage the changes we wish to see. It is important that sustainability advocates and "experts" recognize that we cannot hold out our praise for an "exclusive club" of "perfect" (as if there is such a thing) companies without opening our minds, doors, and wallets to those who are honestly and credibly looking to be better.

The bottom line is the bottom. Some asset managers are deciding it is risky—for both their clients and the planet—to invest in companies with environmentally unsustainable business strategies. The demand for coal to generate electricity is declining. In 2018 nearly every major public oil company faced at least one shareholder resolution about climate change. Those proposals won record shareholder support.

Climate-Action 100+, a group of money managers overseeing more than $33 trillion, works to influence the largest corporate emitters of greenhouse gases. So far, the organization has persuaded Royal Dutch Shell to set short-term climate targets and publish a report on its lobbying of governments. Members backed a shareholder resolution that asked BP to detail how each new capital investment aligns with the Paris Agreement adopted at the United Nations Framework Convention on

Climate Change in 2015. That resolution, supported by BP's management, won the approval of 99 percent of shareholders.[19]

Of course, this would mean nothing if investors were not (as) interested. Increasingly, they are.

While millennials (born between 1977 and 1995) seem to be most interested in applying their ideals on ESG issues to their finances, Gen Xers (1965 to 1976) and baby boomers (1946 to 1964) are also expressing growing interest, per the ESG Investor Sentiment Study[20] from Allianz Life Insurance Company of North America.

The study found that nearly half of Gen Xers and baby boomers say they are interested in having some money in ESG investments, compared with 66 percent of millennials.

When asked to rank the most important issues, all generations expressed that social issues such as diversity in the workforce and consumer protections are most important. This was followed by corporate governance issues and environmental topics.

In addition, as we shall explore in more detail later (Section "Leveraging Your Expertise" in Chapter 4 and Section "The Power of Purpose" in Chapter 5), the majority across all generations say ESG is a key factor in those companies with which they choose to do business (77 percent of millennials/64 percent of Gen Xers/61 percent of boomers).

Discussion Questions

1. Would you put your money into highest-rate-of-return investments even if the companies contradicted your personal values? How would your financial circumstances dictate that decision?

2. Are you a short- or long-term investor?

---

[19]Press Release. n.d. "Socially Responsible Investing and ESG: It's Not Just a Millennial Trend." https://www.businesswire.com/news/home/20190812005374/en/, (accessed August 12, 2019).

[20]Bloomberg. August 7, 2019. "Big Money Starts to Dump Stocks That Pose Climate Risks." https://www.bloomberg.com/news/articles/2019-08-07/big-money-starts-to-dump-stocks-that-pose-climate-risks, (accessed August 9, 2019).

CHAPTER 3

Five Keys to Integrate Sustainability into the Business

Introduction

Most business leaders recognize the need to adapt to maintain their ability to meet changes in the market, the political environment, and public needs. At the same time, however, they are keenly aware of, and will remain committed to, maintaining the core elements that they believe have been responsible for their success in the past. This is the balance that leaders must maintain: remaining true to what differentiates their business while being flexible and nimble enough to predict, embrace, and lead in an ever-changing and competitive world.

As societal expectations change, companies must be prepared to respond. Expectations of what it means to be a "good" corporate citizen have changed so that companies must do more than simply meet statutory requirements in their efforts to satisfy the customers' needs with products and services and their owners' demand for a satisfactory financial return. Increasingly long-term financial success requires business strategies that include good customer and supplier relationships, reducing opposition to growth, enhancing speed to market, fostering a favorable regulatory climate and requirements, and maximizing human resources.

Whether employee safety, environmental stewardship, labor relations, product quality, or community relations—including taxes paid—companies have the power to make this decision. And with the power comes corporate responsibility.

The new "rules" return the emphasis to stakeholders from the shareholder—bringing back the fundamental rule of capitalism. Sustainable companies define customers as the community of stakeholders who impact their business, not just those who purchase their goods or services. And they also are careful to identify who are not customers (or stakeholder)—those for whom the success of the business is secondary, immaterial, or contrary to their agenda.

The new "rules" also focus on empowering employees and igniting their passion for the company and making them part of its success. This ties in with the importance of visionary and courageous leadership and the importance of having a corporate "soul."

First, we shall see how the five value drivers described above can be leveraged to help support an organization's overall strategy, which is essential if sustainability is going to be integrated into the business and not a nice-to-have add-on.

Support the Organization's Overall Strategy

Contrary to popular perception of companies, most successful organizations not only do manage their operations on a quarterly or yearly basis. Successful companies work to balance both short- and long-term goals. Often these are broken into four typical "strategic imperatives"—financial performance, operational efficiency, sales, and cultural imperatives.

In order to ensure these objectives are managed and met, companies often develop strategy maps that are defined, vetted, and approved by its senior leaders.

- Operational—improve efficiency, reduce costs of materials, safety;
- Sales—increase sales of premium products, improve margins;
- Financial—reduce time between delivery and payment, favorable credit terms; and
- Cultural—attract, hire, and retain the best talent, productivity, engagement.

To be an integral part of the company strategy, the sustainability program must be integrated into these established and agreed-upon efforts.

Table 3.1 Conceptual strategy map showing how sustainability value drivers align with typical strategic imperatives. Innovations in service of these organizational goals can be developed in collaboration with the department or team responsible for meeting them.

Business Categories	Sustainability Value Drivers				
	License to Operate	Cost Reduction	Market Opportunity	Employee Engagement	Access to Investment Capital
Financial		▲ Reduce days sales outstanding ▲ Reduce fines		▲ Ensure excellence	▲ Enhance reputation as a good investment ▲ Appeal to growing social responsible investment funds/analysts
Sales	▲ Expand share of business with existing clients ▲ 100 percent retention of existing clients		▲ Increase market share ▲ Expand premium offer ▲ Increase sales volume to existing customers ▲ Attract new customers	▲ Maximize bonus and growth opportunities	▲ Improve margins
Operational	▲ Identify & integrate best practices throughout company ▲ Maximize safety ▲ Ensure compliance	▲ Increase productivity ▲ Reduce waste ▲ Reduce transportation costs ▲ Reduce lost time accidents ▲ Reduce mediation	▲ Provide the best and reliable service ▲ Be responsive to customers	▲ Culture of continuous Improvement	▲ Reduce raw materials costs ▲ Ensure compliance
Cultural	▲ Align HR processes and incentives with desired outcomes	▲ Reduce turnover		▲ Attract / hire / retain / engage the best talent	

Within each of these categories, goals are defined and assigned to various operating units. These are your internal "customers"—and demonstrating how you can help them meet their goals is how the sustainability department (or role) becomes a strategic partner.

Those who wish to "sell it upstairs" (or in the C-suite) know that the best way to do this is to demonstrate how the proposal you are making helps to achieve one (or more) of the objectives that the company leadership has already identified as important and supports one or more of the established goals. Whether developed by yourself or in collaboration with the departments/teams that have responsibility for the strategic imperatives, this is how the innovation high ground (competitive differentiation) can be established.

The measure of success is not how well your business model supports sustainability objectives but rather how well your sustainability efforts support—and help define—your business model.

It is important to note that people in leadership positions often care passionately about and may give generously to social and environmental causes. But when they are sitting at the boardroom table, they are paid to put their personal passions aside and make decisions based on the company's best interests. Therefore, it is imperative that sustainability professionals adopt the language and priorities of the C-suite instead of futilely trying to convince people who are thinking about their business priorities using emotional arguments. This is more than just language and branding. Instead of trying to convince business leaders that corporate responsibility is a "good thing to do," approaching it in this manner demonstrates how it helps move the company in the direction that they already want to go—and every success further integrates the function.

Managers and leaders who recognize that employees are essential for the success of a business are increasingly focused on attracting, hiring, and retaining talent as a "cultural" strategic imperative. With the baby boomer generation reaching retirement age, the number of available workers is declining. At the same time, younger graduates have different values and expectations from employers. While traditionalists may remember the days of corporate pensions and long (30-year) careers with one company, younger workers have no experience with this. Many, facing excellent job prospects, are choosing to favor jobs where they can match a sense of purpose or that meets their desires for improved work–life balance.

Even if the strategy is less formally defined, it is possible to find out what the various departments are working on and realistically identify (there is nothing to gain, and credibility to be lost by overpromising) which efforts can be assisted or even accomplished through sustainability programs. The result will be a program that is integrated into the business and grows—because it is integral to the business and helps it grow.

Discussion Questions

1. Map your sustainability efforts to existing strategies.
2. Who are the key "owners" of the issues identified? Can you work with them for shared success?
3. What strategies have no owner or are foundering? Can you devise a solution?

Compatible with the Day-to-Day Reality

If a sustainability program is to provide value to a company on a regular basis, it must be compatible with the reality that employees face every day. Therefore, things like "best practices" that often focus on operational efficiency and safety must be aligned with sustainability objectives, and vice versa.

Many employees face daily realities, such as customer expectations, that can appear to conflict with corporate sustainability directives. Failing to address and respond to these real or perceived incompatibilities is a key reason why so many corporate initiatives falter.

Sustainability professionals must use their knowledge and understanding of the "on the ground" reality to establish credibility at all levels within the company by developing a strategy that clearly and compellingly communicates how the new programs support and can improve conditions such as by increasing efficiency, reducing overhead costs, and—perhaps most important—meeting customer requirements.

An operating procedure that focuses on speed can be incompatible with safety. Companies know that this is the case and often seek to strike a balance between the two. A true "safety culture" will make that the first imperative, with swiftness second.

But sometimes they are compatible. UPS has received a lot of attention for implementing a simple-sounding program to increase efficiency of deliveries—avoid as many left-hand turns as possible. Because left turns require crossing a lane of oncoming traffic, they are considered more dangerous. In left-hand drive countries, the opposite is the case. In those countries, UPS drivers try to avoid right-hand turns.

Asking people to do something "different" or change procedures in order to be sustainable is a recipe for failure, unless the new procedure is adopted as a standard way of doing business. Since companies are often looking for ways to improve efficiency and save money, initiatives that achieve those objectives and have a social or environmental component (i.e., less waste or fewer accidents) are more easily adopted.

"The most sustainable mile is the one we never drive, so route optimization is an important part of reducing our footprint," says Suzanne Lindsay-Walker, UPS's chief sustainability officer. "On-Road Integrated Optimization and Navigation (ORION), our groundbreaking route optimization software, uses package detail, customized map data, and advanced algorithms to determine the most efficient delivery route for a driver's day."

UPS's latest route optimization efforts, ORION, has combined with earlier efforts, generating annual savings of 100 million miles, 10 million gallons of fuel, and about 100,000 metric tons of emissions.[1]

Empower and Engage Employees at All Levels within the Organization

For many years, the model, particularly in America, has been to make one's fortune and to give back at the end of a hopefully successful and lucrative career and/or to give back during weekends and hours not on the company payroll.

To those who feel passionate about environmental and social issues, this separation of their work and their conscience creates a kind of a

---

[1]ORION   Backgrounder.   https://www.pressroom.ups.com/pressroom/Content DetailsViewer.page?ConceptType=Factsheets&id=1426321616277-282,   (accessed September 30, 2019).

"Bruce Wayne/Batman paradox" because people often recognize that their actions during their career are at best unrelated but at worst are *negatively contributing* to the same causes that they are addressing during their nonwork hours. Hypothetically speaking, examples would be if a business were to host a volunteer event for employees at a local food bank while paying its employees so poorly that some of them might be relying on that assistance for their own needs, or if a local clean-up event were to include employees picking up litter branded with their company logo.

Some companies have engaged in organized philanthropy and volunteerism efforts designed to allow employees to do good works on their company time. This often builds a greater sense of loyalty and team as senior executives' participation in these events provides access for employees who might not otherwise gain entree into having a conversation with their corporate leaders.

But when done well, like the industry-leading partnership formed between construction materials producer Lafarge and Habitat for Humanity International, the impact on employees affirms the role the business (and its products or services) plays in the community. "This provides are great opportunity for us to see how our product is used and to see the corporation as a whole and some of what it gets involved with," said Jack Francis of the Palatka Gypsum Plant. Tom Millwee of the Roberta Cement Plant appreciated "Lafarge donating the materials and giving me the opportunity to work on this project."

Just as this sense of ownership is a powerful incentive, the opposite is also true. Lack of ownership may lead employees to compromise the effort, either deliberately or unintentionally. A classic example is a power-saving effort that automates temperature control but is not flexible enough to accommodate employees who work outside regular hours. Using fans or space heaters to make themselves comfortable (certainly understandable) is a sign that your employees have not been made part of the program.

As with any culture defining effort, a truly integrated sustainability culture requires the individual buy-in and the empowerment of everyone in the company as well as changes in processes and procedures, including training.

Success cannot rely on the work of a designated team of experts to carry the ball for the organization. Everyone has to participate if it is to become part of the corporate culture. Leaders in corporate responsibility offer employees training that goes beyond technical skills such as processes and procedures and safety in the workplace to areas including management skills, diversity and inclusion, influencing without authority, etc. Companies that are serious about this make these trainings compulsory and link advancement opportunities to those who have demonstrated the core values in action. Most people, and companies, approach the fact that in a rapidly changing world, lifelong learning is essential to have and maintain a career. And it is also necessary for a company to stay competitive. The old management joke applies:

Manager: What if we train our employees and they leave?
Second manager: What if we don't and they stay?

Employees are more than just members of an organization. They are also members of, and represent, the community where the business operates. Often, they are the first to hear honest feedback about public perceptions of the company, and its actions, before management does (especially in organizations that have a headquarters and geographically dispersed operations).

What many organizations fail to recognize is that employees, whether they wear the logo on their uniform, hard hat, ball cap, or other corporate "swag," are ambassadors in the community. They represent the company not only in settings where they may be asked to present the company, but informally every day by their actions and words. Some companies seek to restrict their employees' activities on digital media, never appreciating that they have the same (or even greater) impact when they are on their own personal time and someone asks about the company, or they engage in behavior while wearing the company apparel. Companies are so sanguine about corporate swag that they often give it away (at public events) without worrying how people might act while wearing it.

But companies that provide their employees with even minimal training on a few key messages can leverage the power of their workforce in those informal settings. It can be every bit as defining for a company brand as the interactions during the course of their business day. While most employees are not experienced community engagement professionals, they are very credible experts in their areas of expertise. Having them participate in events like school "career days" not only allows the company to have representatives in the community, but also helps employees to reengage with the value of what they do day to day and how it impacts peoples' lives (see Chapter 5, Section "The Power of Purpose").

Just as employees who learn CPR and First Aid have come to assist coworkers (and others) in their times of distress, training employees about aspects of diversity and inclusion can help them in their day-to-day interactions. Stories about people defusing incidents of harassment in public can help an organization improve its reputation if the person who engaged in the correct helpful actions mentions that they learned about how to deal with those incidents at work. (Conversely, incidents that are poorly handled [such as a person or group of one ethnicity being asked to leave a coffee shop] demonstrate a company that has failed to adequately train its employees in both the company's values and the techniques to use.)

Many companies have Employee Network Groups that invite people to join to help mentor others. Those groups can be based on gender, race, military veteran status, generation, sexual identity, orientation, etc. Those groups provide an opportunity for not only learning but also employee engagement and serve as a tangible demonstration of the company's values. If those groups host or participate in public events, it provides another mechanism for community outreach and engagement. "I never expected our company to be a sponsor of the Capital PRIDE parade," recounted an employee at that event. "But I was even more surprised to see how many of my coworkers—and company leadership—joined in."

Starbucks uses the term "partner" rather than ambassadors for those employees that they have designated to promote the company socially. Starbucks is a more prescribed effort. The company provides detailed guidelines regarding what "partners" should—and should not—do when posting on behalf of the company. This increases the employees' sense of belonging, but it also emphasizes their accountability for the content they post on the company's behalf.

According to Starbucks CEO Howard Shultz:

[Employees] are the true ambassadors of our brand, the real merchants of romance, and as such the primary catalysts for delighting customers. [Employees] elevate the experience for each customer – something you can hardly accomplish with a billboard or a 30-second spot.[2]

Lastly, absolutely nothing is more antithetical to a culture than when employees who do not live the values are nevertheless promoted. Those who meet their financial targets but who flaunt (whether actively or passively) the cultural values are, as Jack Welch, former CEO of General Electric said, the most *dangerous* to the culture because these high-flyers are seen as proof that profit, more than values, is the key to success.[3]

Bosses at every level too often sell out and go for the short-term results over the behaviors. Indeed, most of us have probably been guilty somewhere along the way of letting the burning desire for good results cover up the sins....

Discussion Questions

1. Have you ever seen someone who was undeserving get promoted/rewarded? How did that impact your morale?

2. If someone performs at a high level and is popular but acted in a manner that did not support the culture, what would you do? Assume no laws or corporate policies were being broken.

Provide Tangible, Measurable Results

Businesspeople are about results. Are we selling more than we did last week/month/quarter/year? Did we make the budget number? Did we meet market expectations? Are our customers reporting satisfaction and returning?

---

[2]H. Shultz. 2012. *Onward: How Starbucks Fought for Its Life without Losing Its Soul* (New York, NY: Rodale Books). https://www.amazon.com/Onward-Starbucks-Fought-without-Losing/dp/1609613821.

[3]J. Welch. 2015. "Winning, Do You Have a Jerk Employee Problem? How to Deal with It." https://jackwelch.strayer.edu/winning/jerk-employee-problem, (accessed August 25, 2019).

At the outset, it is better to focus on those smaller, quick wins that establish your credibility that what you are doing is actually driving the business, whether it is helping the corporate reputation, reducing costs, or changing our reputation in the community. Those things become the things that the C-suite is looking for. Success engenders requests for more; then it becomes a conversation of what else sustainability can help achieve.

That is why the most successful sustainability programs are designed by a coalition including internal stakeholders from strategy, finance, supply chain, marketing, risk management, strategy, and customer relations in addition to the more typically expected stakeholder in human resources, environment, and the safety functions.

Beyond an internal coalition, sustainability professionals often use "materiality assessments" to help identify an organization's most "material issues" and determine what should be a priority by capturing both internal and external perspectives. The process of identifying these issues involves reaching out to internal and external stakeholders to get their input. While time-consuming, it is a huge opportunity to gain buy-in on how you'll measure success.

Ideally materiality assessments can (and should) inform both strategy and reporting. Many organizations use them as the basis for their sustainability reports.

The key to getting real value out of any materiality assessment is starting with a clear understanding of what information you are looking for. This enables you to ask the right questions, choose the right stakeholders, apply the appropriate methodology, and visually present the information effectively to help inform decisions.

Part of this is demonstrating that the issues identified in the materiality assessment have direct linkages and impacts to the operational, sales, financial, and cultural imperatives discussed earlier. At the same time, reaching out to external stakeholders provides an opportunity to cross-reference those imperatives with the issues of concern to your stakeholders.

When ranked on a scale of 1 to 10 (with 1 being the least and 10 the most important), the issues can be mapped using a chart, where the internal assessment of priority is along a horizontal (or X) axis and the importance assigned to the issue defines placement on a vertical (or Y) axis. This will help you to define the moderate, high, and very high priorities, based on how many elements fall where on the chart (Figure 3.1).

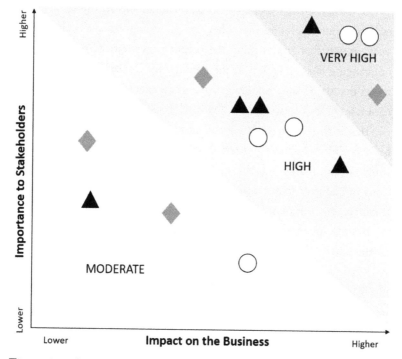

Figure 3.1 A materiality assessment graphically illustrates the issues that are most important to both internal and external stakeholders. The "must do" items are in the upper right. Once those are being addressed, working on the issues in the middle band is often considered differentiating, because most of the "must do" items are likely being addressed by others in the business sector as well

In this version, different colors and shapes have been used to indicate what could be environmental, social, and governance issues. This visual difference also helps show patterns, because this is a lot of information in one place. But putting both company and stakeholder priorities together enables the senior leaders to see the relative importance of issues to the business and how public perception may differ at the same time.

A well-crafted materiality assessment can inform both reporting and strategy. From a strategy or business case standpoint, the goal is to prioritize what an organization can and should do. But from a reputation standpoint, it is important to realize that items that are both "high" for stakeholders and the company are likely to be considered "the cost of doing business" or necessary. Therefore, from a reputation standpoint, addressing items in the middle band—the ones you and your stakeholders both rank as being important but less vital—is what helps define leadership. That is where an organization can often find its "value proposition" because they are doing more than what is deemed necessary, and that differentiates them.

As we saw earlier, the Monks and Lajoux research has shown the business case for, and impact of, enhancing the reputation of one's organization based on what stakeholders consider important.

Different Kinds of Targets

There are several different kinds of targets that seek to measure absolute, intensity, percentage, plan referenced, past referenced, and programmatic.

Each of these has its strengths and its weaknesses. But agreeing on how you are going to measure performance is essential.

Absolute targets focus on the true total impact, the number of trees planted, the total amount of CO_2e greenhouse gas emissions avoided, or the amount of water consumed in a process. There is a tendency to think of absolute targets as "better" because they measure what is actually emitted, spent, produced, saved, etc. But if an organization grows, their absolute numbers may immediately go up as a consequence; and that creates a paradox. If a company has committed to reduce emissions but adds new operations (through an acquisition) it may have to report an overall increase in net emissions of *their* operations. If they are committed to reducing emissions and the new operations are now brought under their operational control and subject to the same efforts, that would be a *net benefit* in reducing impacts that were not being reduced before. But if they were to build something new, instead of taking over an existing operation, that would be a net increase. This is why some organizations that intend to grow may shy away from absolute targets.

Intensity targets are based on per unit. It allows for comparison between like things. Familiar examples include unit pricing on groceries or miles per gallon for automobiles. It is a good way to measure improved efficiency, reduced energy use, lower emissions, etc. For things like operational excellence, these kinds of targets focus on "best practices" without causing issues relating to changes in growth that absolute targets can create.

Percentage targets allow a company to set a percent change based on an established baseline year. This can include a percent reduction in emissions, energy use, or waste or growth—such as the balance of women or minorities in leadership positions.

Plan referenced targets are often used when rolling out a new program. They focus on the target (such as "We will implement our safety program in 100 percent of operations" by a certain year) or milestones set along the way ("We will replace 25 percent of our lightbulbs with LEDs by year 1, 50 percent by year 2 and 100 percent by year 3"). These measures track how a plan is being implemented but do not give correlated impact results.

Programmatic targets are similar, but often focus on continuing established efforts rather than something new, such as "our employees will receive a minimum of 5 hours of diversity training a year."

Past referenced are similar, but based not on the plan but rather on where a company was when it began its efforts: "We will cut our accident rate from X to Y" and again with a specified time frame in which the goal will be reached or "we will replace 25 diesel busses with natural gas or electric a year for the next five years." These kinds of targets, while accurate expressions of actions and results, are quickly falling out of favor because measuring from the past does not give a clear indication of progress toward a goal.

What Is Tangible Based on Benefits to the Business

There are different kinds of results. The most obvious are those tangible results that benefit the business. There are also earlier implementation goals, such as measuring your efforts and results in rolling out a new program, that are necessary precursors to the impact results.

Most people do not fear change—what they fear are the unforeseen negative consequences of change. Instead of presenting the idea of sustainability as a radical transformation of their core enterprise, a review of the foundational documents of the organization often provides ample evidence that building an enduring business model is a natural extension of the values that were responsible for its success in the first place.

Whether through independent third-party certifications (such as EnergyStar for energy efficiency, organic for certain foods, etc.), recognized and respected awards, or reporting against trusted criteria, the public is skeptical of unsubstantiated claims, as are employees. In some cases, it is easy to point to results—wildlife habitats set aside are visible examples within a community that a company and its employees can see for themselves. That is why local examples are very powerful.

Even those at a distance can be made real through photographs and stories of the good that is being done. But in some cases, it is harder because you are quantifying what did not happen—energy saved, trees that were not cut down, water that was not used, etc. In those cases, the use of social math—equating it to things that people can relate—is powerful. Gallons of water saved can be compared to the number of swimming pools it would fill. Power savings can be related to the number of homes' worth of electricity saved, etc.

For management, for measurable results to really be considered tangible, they must tie back to the organization's strategy (as explained earlier). Showing quantifiable business results offers the opportunity to demonstrate that programs are working for the benefit of the entire organization.

Consider the impacts of having more customers switch to electronic billing and payment, rather than mailings back and forth. For the company, this may be a financial imperative because in addition to the cost of printing and processing those invoices, a company can also save the staff time associated with mailing, collecting, and depositing the payments. However, customers may be more motivated by completely different criteria, such as looking at ways to reduce their own environmental footprint.

About a third of the customers of a Washington DC-based company participated in electronic billing, payment, or both. Based on the cost per customer mailing, it was determined that a 2 percent increase (from 33 to 35 percent) would result in a net savings of over a quarter million dollars per year. Using social math to determine equivalencies, the Sustainability Department established that the amount of paper used for the billings was just a bit more than 2,200 trees—which happened to be more than the number of Japanese Cherry Trees that surround the Tidal Basin and Jefferson Memorials.

The Sustainability Department proposed an outreach campaign with Customer Experience to help them reach their Paperless Billing goal focusing on the number of trees saved as a pride point during the month of April (2019), which not only includes Earth Day, but also the annual Cherry Blossom Festival. The campaign included e-bill "thank you" messages, paper bills with "join in the effort" inserts, e-mails, hold messages, digital media outreach via the company Twitter account and LinkedIn page, as well as ads in local newspapers. The results showed that e-billing customer rate increased to more than 38 percent and a similar increase in electronic payments (which gets the money into the company faster).

The time value of money (TVM) principle teaches that money available now is worth more than the identical sum in the future due to its potential earning capacity. This core principle of finance holds that, provided money can earn interest, any amount of money is worth more the sooner it is received. That is why getting in payments faster is imperative, especially in lower-margin businesses. Some businesses charge late fees (usually a percentage) to encourage on-time payments. That value add is in addition to the avoided costs from mailings the company did not have to make.

This program had both a percentage target and an associated absolute cost savings.

Another example of this is a program for Lafarge Construction Materials. Some customers were very delinquent in paying—more than 90 days in a few cases. By simply empowering company delivery drivers to offer "Do you have anything I can take back with me?" when they handed in bills, each time they delivered construction aggregates to job sites it encouraged customers to prepare payments and have them ready when their next delivery was due. Originally the concept was to save the 4 or 5 days that the payment would be in the mail, but adding the phrase "It will save you a stamp" ensured that the message was perceived as friendly and not chiding and resulted in some payment delays being shortened by more than a month (in the most extreme example).

This is an example of aligning benefits to the business with benefits to the customer. In this case, the money the customer saved was marginal, but the perceived benefit was of exemplary service (and not bill collection).

Benefits to Customers

"Net gains" is the concept that something that benefits one group can also benefit another. For the above examples, improved customer service (e-billing and avoiding having to mail payments) have benefits to both the business and the customer. Customers also benefit psychologically when they feel good about the products or services that they buy. As we shall see in Section "Earning Passionate Customers" in Chapter 5, there are powerful ways that customers can feel good about purchasing sustainable products from companies that align with their personal values.

Research shows that there is little risk, and much to be gained, when a company takes a moral stand. Automobile manufacturers were widely praised for resisting recent U.S. government efforts to roll back fuel efficiency standards by a public that recognizes and appreciates the benefits of greater gas mileage vehicles—whether they are motivated to save fuel costs, reduce air pollution, or address climate change. General Motors, Ford, BMW, and Toyota (among others) publicly complained that the plans to weaken car pollution and fuel efficiency standards would actually hurt their bottom lines.

The *Business & Politics Do They Mix?* study by Global Strategy Group found that 81 percent of Americans believe corporations should take action to address important issues facing society, and 88 percent believe corporations have the power to influence social change.[4] A company should take a stance if the issue makes sense for the business and to read 'makes sense for the business and is aligned with the company's core values. You may alienate some, but if speaking up brings you closer to your mission, that should be okay in the long term. Ultimately, being aligned and vocal on a social issue can help an organization define and strengthen its true self and connect more deeply with stakeholders.

Benefit to Community

Similarly, benefits to the company often result in benefits to the overall community. Efforts to reduce waste, pollute less, improve safety, etc., benefit all members of the community and not just employees. Companies can save money and gain goodwill by engaging in and reporting the results of efforts such as donating "gently used" office and computer equipment to local not-for-profit organizations (rather than recycling or, even worse, landfilling).

---

[4]Global Strategy Group. 2016. "Business & Politics Do They Mix?" http://www .globalstrategygroup.com/wp-content/uploads/2016/12/2016-GSG-Business-and-Politics_Do-They-Mix_Fourth-Annual-Study.pdf, (accessed August 29, 2019).

Science-Based Targets

The Paris agreement in 2015 saw 195 of the world's governments commit to prevent dangerous climate change by limiting global warming to well below 2°C. This signaled an acceleration in the transition to a low-carbon economy. But science is not absolute and, as our understanding increases, so has the imperative. Targets adopted by companies to reduce greenhouse gas emissions are considered "science based" if they are in line with what the latest climate science says is necessary to meet the goals of the Paris Agreement—to limit global warming to well below 2°C above preindustrial levels and pursue efforts to limit warming to 1.5°C.

The Science-Based Targets Initiative (sciencebasedtargets.org) is a collaboration between CDP, the United Nations Global Compact (UNGC), World Resources Institute (WRI), the World Wildlife Fund for Nature (WWF), and others that hopes to make science-based targets the global standard by 2020. Today more than 600 companies are taking action based on the current science and more than 200 have had their goals certified as being in line with that science. What can be more tangible and worthy of measurement (and reporting) than efforts that are based on the latest science?

Maximize Stakeholder Engagement

The connection between sustainability programs and corporate communications efforts is more than a philosophical one. Because of the strong and increasing importance that employees, customers, clients, and communities place on the environmental, social, and economic impacts an organization has, many of the duties traditionally assigned to company's communications departments to build internal buy-in (organizational culture and employee engagement) and reputational capital (external, community, and public relations) can best be accomplished by maximizing the effective development, implementation, management, and communication of CSR efforts across a company.

The changing information needs of both stakeholders and companies are redefining the role of corporate communications departments and professionals including community, investor, government, and employee relations. Companies are recognizing that, while some people are less discerning about what they read (and share) online, a growing number of increasingly savvy stakeholders are becoming more and more skeptical about messages that corporations are sharing.

The internet has fundamentally transformed not only how people get their information but also the relationship that they have with the information. Instead of passive audiences, those who make their living in communications have the opportunity—and increasingly the obligation—to engage with our stakeholders in open, transparent, and direct conversation as part of a comprehensive communications strategy.

Digital media offer many of the same characteristics—immediacy, transparency, and interactivity—that make one-to-one the most effective form of communication. Progressive companies have recognized the true power of the stakeholder engagement and have made the transition, revising their strategy from sharing information with a passive audience to actively engaging with both internal and external stakeholders. They find that it provides them with an unparalleled opportunity to understand, and respond when appropriate, to what is being said about their enterprise—positive, negative, and neutral.

Companies that wish to build, maintain, or defend their reputations and brand equity have no choice but to join the dialogue, bringing authenticity and transparency to the conversation.

As Julie Starr, founder and managing partner of the Taiga Company and author of *The Business Sustainability Handbook*, puts it, "It's like when you Photoshop life. It might be a beautiful image, but it's not real." She encourages companies to understand that what engages people (be they employees, customers, communities, etc.) is when companies are not afraid and let down their walls and communicate authentically and honestly.

It therefore is critical that a company not be perfect, but rather that it endeavor to act in alignment with its articulated values and, by not being afraid to admit when it falls short, increase its reputation for honesty.

Starr goes further, pointing out that in some cases, "Imperfections are what inspire capture human hearts and inspire us to be more than what we have been in the past. So, imperfections are beautifully embraced."

Discussion Questions

1. Review your targets to determine what type of measurement they are.

2. Are they (all) compatible with your organization's current situation? Do they support its strategy going forward?

3. How will changes to your organization (i.e., growth, acquisitions) impact your targets?

4. Are there targets that are up for renewal?

Table 3.2 *Worksheet for evaluating and updating existing sustainability targets. This combines target setting, strategic alignment, internal stakeholders or "owners" of the strategic imperative, as well as an evaluation of the kind of target and space for updating or drafting a new target*

Sustainability target		
Category		
☐ Energy	☐ Water	☐ Waste
☐ Carbon	☐ Biodiversity/Habitat	☐ Other:
Business strategy alignment(s)	**Owner**	**Secondary**
Cost Savings		
Revenue Generation		
Operational Excellence		
Cultural		
Existing target		
Type of target		
☐ Absolute	☐ Percentage	☐ Past Referenced
☐ Plan Referenced	☐ Context	☐ Programmatic
Target assessment		
☐ Leading Edge	☐ Solid Performer	☐ Falling Out of Favor
New/Modified target		

CHAPTER 4

Creating a Leading Program

Any business, if it wants to be sustained over time, must maximize its profits but do so in a manner that meets the needs of the stakeholders that allow it to remain successful. When those needs change, businesses have a responsibility to adapt their behaviors accordingly. At the same time, as we have seen, strict legal compliance is not a leadership position, because doing so can only put the organization "in with the pack." This also fails to recognize that when any company in a sector fails to meet its obligations in a spectacular fashion (such as the 2010 Deepwater Horizon Oil Spill), the entire industry is tainted by the same brush.

Employees want more than a paycheck.

Communities want the company to be a good corporate citizen and hire from the community, provide employees with a living wage, not pollute and to pay its fair share of taxes, and support the community (even if each of these things is not legally required).

As much as people claim that **shareholders** are only interested in maximizing short-term returns, as we have seen in the section on Attracting Investment Capital in Chapter 2, this too is evolving.

Regulators may only require companies to toe the legal line, but things like sloppy paperwork and cutting it too close to the edge (when it comes to things like environmental impacts or safety) result in more frequent and deeper investigations, costing the company time and money. Having robust systems in place ensure high standards are followed, also resulting in less costly enforcement actions.

In order to lead in the eyes of ever-important **customers**, innovations in products and services must be rapid, without betraying the core "value proposition" that people have come to expect (Figure 4.1).

Influence			Actions				Expertise			
How our values are integrated into business decisions			How we demonstrate our values through our business				How we encourage others to adopt			
• Brand promise – our values guide with whom we do business • Be the benchmark for excellence			• Our culture as differentiator • Brand promise – to maintain the highest standards • Be the benchmark for Operational Excellence				• Leverage the strength of our people • Brand promise – helping others live their values			
←	←	←	Promise	Plan	Program	Performance	→	→	→	→
Business practices (labor, diversity & inclusion, etc.)	Business Sector / Industry	Supply chain	Aspirational Commitments	• Goals • Timelines • Milestones	• Initiatives • Programs • Efforts	• Measurement • Public Reporting • Third party validations	Drive client actions	Encourage customer decisions	Increase public awareness/expectations	Facilitate behavior change

Figure 4.1 The Actions–Influence–Expertise framework offers a way to visualize the company's efforts. This is useful for both planning and stakeholder engagement, because it clearly shows areas in the value change (both suppliers and customers) where the company can take actions that demonstrate how it lives its values beyond its own operations

Your ability to drive behaviors is strongest with your own organization (your "footprint") and becomes more challenging as you move from those you "touch" directly (your "handprint") to those organizations and individuals who are "under your shadow" of impact.

Integrating Sustainability into Your Actions

The first way that organizations must establish their leadership is through their own actions—and one can argue that this is the bare minimum. However, this can be hard for larger organizations that may have entrenched methods of doing things, because it requires that one's actions continually evolve, but that the underlying basis for those actions—the values that define the organization—remain rock solid and consistent.

Companies that lead are not afraid to experiment with new ideas and are willing (and in fact eager) to challenge their existing perceptions on a regular basis. Leaders in sustainability are not looking for ways to hang on to existing practices; they are investing new programs and models that reduce the use of energy and natural resources. Sometimes they even set long-range targets without knowing exactly how they will achieve them. But announcing their intention often generates the internal enthusiasm (and sometimes external pressure) necessary to drive real changes.

In 2016 Washington Gas announced that it had exceeded its two aggressive greenhouse gas reduction goals. Using a 2008 baseline year the company pledged to reduce emissions from its fleet and facilities by 70 percent and the emissions intensity of the gas it delivered to customers by 18 percent by 2020.

"When we set the targets, we were challenged by our CEO to aim higher, so we had a plan to get about 80 percent of the way there," admits Melissa E. Adams, the company's chief corporate social responsibility officer. "But with the support of leadership, and the structure of an annual incentive program that included the actions necessary, we were confident we would make it."

The actions necessary to meet the targets included projects like a new LEED-certified building and accelerated pipeline replacement programs. Those efforts were integrated into the company's Corporate Scorecard, which is tied directly to the annual bonus for employees. But the "stretch" target also encouraged innovative thoughts and ideas as people "got into it." By 2014, Washington Gas had achieved a 74 percent reduction in absolute greenhouse gas emissions from its fleet and facilities and a 20 percent reduction in methane emissions for every unit of natural gas delivered, readily beating both targets ahead of schedule.

In its press release the company also included the fact that an independent third party had validated their results, which is another way to validate results and enhance credibility among a sometimes skeptical public.[1]

The company also set new targets: for its fleet and facilities to be carbon neutral by 2025 and to further reduce the emissions intensity of the gas to a total of 38 percent from its original baseline, emission reductions in line with the "well below 2 degrees C" goal determined at the COP21 meeting (aka "The Paris Agreement"). Adams' determination and forward thinking are palpable when she says:

> This will be achieved through innovative programs that underscore our mission to be responsible stewards of the environment, deliver clean energy solutions that lower emissions for our customers, and reduce energy costs.

A target based on a company's existing business plans is less challenging, and therefore less impressive, to both external stakeholders and employees. As Ruben Rodriguez said in the video the company released featuring employees explaining why beating the target made them proud (to work there), "I'm proud for how we recognized the challenge and overcame it."[2]

Another example of letting the aspiration drive the innovation is UPS, with their "Rolling Laboratory." They are experimenting using a diverse fleet of more than 10,000 alternative fuel and advanced technology

---

[1]WGL Holdings. 2016. "Washington Gas Exceeds Carbon Reduction Goals Four Years Ahead of Schedule." https://www.businesswire.com/news/home/20160922005143/en/Washington-Gas-Exceeds-Carbon-Reduction-Goals-Years (accessed February 10, 2020).

[2]WGL. 2016. "We're Proud of 70." https://www.youtube.com/watch?v=QuwnuvOv8JQ&list=PLHAZSJ84PKJRVfHJX29UoUZP0nGqbkpLf&index=11&t=0s, (accessed September 11, 2019).

vehicles in 13 countries. These vehicles range from electrically assisted tricycles such as Cargo Cruisers in city centers for trips of less than 20 miles to propane-powered trucks for rural routes of 100 miles. For even longer trips, between 400 and 600 miles, they are using biomethane or renewable natural gas-powered trucks. This specialized fleet drives more than 1 million cleaner miles each business day.[3] In 2018, UPS purchased 119 million gallons of alternative fuels, which represents 22 percent of total ground fuel usage.[4]

In an article in Fleet Equipment Magazine, UPS explained that not every innovation works, and not all work for their needs (high turnover, many miles, stop and go driving). "Although all projects do not result in large scale deployments, they give us valuable experience for future decisions," explains Bill Brentar, senior director of maintenance and engineering for transportation equipment.[5]

The cement industry is responsible for a large amount of carbon emissions because CO_2 is released as part of the cement-making process. The industry is responding through a consortium that is made up of cement and lime producers, and research and development institutions, LEILAC (Low Emissions Intensity Lime and Cement).

Norcem and HeidelbergCement Northern Europe have publicly stated a vision of zero emissions of CO_2 from concrete products by 2030. They are working on several carbon-capture initiatives including a promising pilot program at the HeidelbergCement plant in Lixhe, Belgium. Technology from Australian technology company Calix that separates and captures CO_2 is being adapted in an effort to capture the CO_2 produced by the cement manufacturing process.[6]

[3]UPS. 2019. "Environmental Responsibility." https://sustainability.ups.com/sustainability-strategy/environmental-responsibility, (accessed September 30, 2019).

[4]UPS. 2018. "Goals and Progress: 2018 Progress Toward Our Aspirations,." https://sustainability.ups.com/progress-report/goals-and-progress/, (accessed September 13, 2019).

[5]J. Morgan. 2018. "Inside the UPS Rolling Laboratory," *Fleet Equipment*. https://www.fleetequipmentmag.com/the-rolling-laboratory/, (accessed September 13, 2019).

[6]C. Beumelburg. 2016. "Breakthrough Technology for Carbon Capture." https://www.heidelbergcement.com/en/leilac-research-project, (accessed August 30, 2019).

We currently have a linear economy. A linear economy is one that uses natural resources to produce goods. It may take years, decades, or even centuries, but eventually things that are finite will always run out. Efforts to reduce, reuse, and recycle all slow the rate of consumption, but there is only so far that you can extend finite—although they may be vast—resources. It is a mathematical certainty.

That is why there is such a focus on renewable resources: things that replenish themselves. The idea is to slow consumption below the rates that things regenerate. The challenge is, of course, a growing population driving increasing demand. Increasing awareness of this challenge is the concept behind "Earth Overshoot Day."

Each year the Global Footprint Network, an international sustainability think tank, calculates the date when humanity's demand for ecological resources (trees removed from forests or fish caught for food, for instance) in a given year exceeds what Earth can regenerate in that year. The days between Overshoot Day and the actual end of the year make up the "environmental deficit"—the amount we are drawing down the Earth's natural reserves.

The promise of renewable resources is that if we lower our consumption rate below that of the replenishment rate, we will never run out. But all our efforts that focus on efficiency—and shifting from nonrenewable to renewable resources—have not stopped the inexorable progress of Overshoot Day earlier and earlier each year. The fact that it keeps getting earlier shows that we're not only catching up to the "end of the road," we're also increasing the rate we're approaching that "milestone." That is why efficiency is only a partial answer.

In contrast, a circular economy takes in goods at the end of their useful life cycle and uses them as the raw materials to either recreate them (like recycling paper) or for new products (like tires becoming asphalt). When the "end" of one life cycle is also the "beginning" of another, one can carry on infinitely, like a road that reconnects back to itself.

Beyond reducing our consumption of finite resources (and helping to get us under the "overshoot" of renewable resources), the promise and power of developing a circular economy is the ability to continue to meet the needs of people (and expanding the progress we have made toward longevity and quality of life) in a way that is sustainable.

Other examples include companies that are extracting the petroleum from discarded plastic bottles and using it to create the polyester fibers that they turn into sportswear. Pentatonic makes all of its furniture from post-consumer waste. The company also recycles its own products into new products at the end of useful life.

Using Your Influence to Advance Sustainability (Supply Chain, Industry, and Business Standards)

The concept "not in my backyard" has become obsolete because, in our globally connected world, it becomes impossible to ignore that everyone's backyard is someone else's front yard.

As we have seen earlier, brand reputation is an important value driver for businesses. In reputation and brand management, companies that insist that suppliers meet rigorous sustainable business standards are protected from damage to their brand and reputation from issues such as child labor, substandard wages, environmental mismanagement, etc. And they are helping prevent these practices by providing a financial incentive—their business—for acting in a socially responsible manner.

Leaders know that they need to look beyond their own actions and values, beyond those things over which they control to those things over which they can exert influence, such as their supply chains. This includes holding suppliers to adhere to values relating to human rights, working and labor conditions, living wages, environmental stewardship, and governance issues. Companies recognize that they cannot outsource problems in an effort to distance themselves from their negative impacts—as BP discovered when it attempted to lay the blame for the Deepwater Horizon disaster at the feet of the companies it had selected to work on its behalf. Similarly, after a rash of vehicles surging out of Park and causing accidents, Toyota could not credibly argue it held a core value of safety by attempting to blame problems with the throttle mechanisms built for them by a different company.

Companies are requiring suppliers to do more than guarantee a level of quality for the products that they supply; some are requiring that suppliers maintain a chain of custody to ensure that the products that they are using conform to environmental and social values as well. Large power purchasers have been exploring the extent of the influence that they can have on their suppliers' behavior by implementing requirements beyond prices. Examples include Walmart's efforts to only sell certified sustainable seafood. To be a supplier to Walmart, the giant retailer must be convinced—using third-party validation—that the seafood products that they are being offered to sell to customers are, in fact, sourced from sustainable species, caught only in places where those fish are plentiful, and that they are being fished in a responsible manner.

The new focus on a "sustainable" economy is creating opportunities for companies that offer products or services that help other companies reduce their environmental impacts, and even those that track information back to point, country, or company of origin. A great example is in information technology, which can be used not only to help improve efficiencies in manufacturing but also to look at entire systems and provide vital information. In day-to-day application, measurement devices that monitor traffic flow can be used to automatically adjust traffic lights to facilitate safety and efficiency of transportation. Buildings that install monitors of electric power use help manage the peaks and valleys in consumption, reducing energy costs and helping utilities determine where and when power is needed. Devices that measure the depth and speed of rivers can be used to feed real-time data that can protect lives and property from natural disasters such as floods.

Moving beyond the environmental pillar, on the social side, experts in issues like global development, fair trade, workers' rights, and labor relations will also continue to be in demand, because companies are increasingly going to be asked (required) to measure and report on their footprints in these areas as well.

"Considerations about sustainability in the supply chain are no longer optional. In all regions of the world, these issues are front and center of both the business and political agenda," wrote Tim Mohin, chief executive of the Global Reporting Initiative (GRI) in May 2019.[7]

---

[7]T. Mohin. 2019. "Supply Chain Transparency Is a Business Necessity." https://medium.com/@GlobalReportingInitiative/supply-chain-transparency-is-a-business-necessity-b88451a9a6ef, (accessed August 12, 2019).

Mohin acknowledges that transparency is not the first instinct for a business when it comes to their supply chain. After all, that is often where they obtain essential materials and products that mark their competitive differentiation. But when it is not managed effectively or appropriately, a supply chain can also contain a great deal of risk. And risk must also be managed. As Mohin writes, "it's essential to track the origin of products and services for their environmental and human rights implications."

In the 1990s Nike sought to distance itself from conditions in its suppliers' factories. This created a crisis for the brand because the company was making purchasing decisions based on values that were different than those it stated when it faced customers. Even when completely compliant with local laws and regulations, transparency enabled by the Internet meant that a company could hide the conditions, labor practices, etc., in its supply chain and it was held morally, if not legally, accountable.

Thanks to the Internet and social media, events that take place a world away are brought to our collective consciousness with such an immediacy and authenticity that companies may be ill prepared to face. The concept "not in my backyard" has become obsolete because, in our globally connected world, it becomes impossible to ignore that everyone's backyard is someone else's front yard. That means those things a company may wish to hide (or may not even be aware of being done on its behalf) are a mouse-click away from going viral and ending up on the evening news, Twitter, or at the next shareholder meeting.

Mohin goes on:

Dealing with supply chain risks can help minimize disruption from environmental and social impacts while protecting the company brand. Also, ensuring suppliers have effective compliance programs and robust management systems can enhance the reliability and efficiency of the supply chain, which adds value to the business.

Transparency based on good data is the foundation of good supply chain management. Companies manage what they measure, which is why monitoring the key impacts is essential for efficient and sustainable supply chains.

The power of public reporting is not just in knowing, it is the drive to improve.

Another incentive ties back to license to operate. Regulators are less likely to impose new rules when evolving standards are already being met. In other words, companies voluntarily holding themselves to higher-than-legal-requirement standards can prevent regulations from being imposed (and the associated costs of documenting compliance). Mandates for supply chain transparency are increasing. Both the UK and Australia are now requiring reporting on efforts to confront and prevent modern slavery. As electronics companies rely on rare materials for their products, increasing concerns about "conflict minerals"—raw materials sourcing that may contribute to human rights abuses and even war—are rising. Can/will regulation be far behind?

As Mohin states, "The trend is clear: well managed businesses have strong supplier responsibility programs. And these are the businesses that win in the global economy."

Leveraging Your Expertise to Change Customers and Communities (Making Them Want and Favor Sustainable Products and Services)

The last way that people expect companies to demonstrate leadership is by using their expertise. Beyond the niche consumer segment that will always seek out and is willing to pay more for goods and services that match their values, the clear majority of consumers must be driven to action through more traditional value drivers for those goods or services. For example, the ultimate success of electric vehicles will depend on other attributes as much as their reduced environmental impacts. By offering aesthetic appeal, performance, safety, reliability, and the waiver that allows such vehicles to use the express lanes in some jurisdictions, those vehicles will have greater appeal, because they will offer benefits that matter to a wider range of automotive purchasers.

Programs such as charging and refunding deposits on glass and plastic bottles and aluminum cans to provide direct financial incentives for desired behaviors can be successful, but they often have limited impact when convenience and comfort needs are not met. When Home Depot creates a mechanism for people to bring back used compact fluorescent light bulbs (to prevent them from going into landfills) or when auto repair facilities take back worn-out car batteries, those are attempts to influence consumer behavior. In these cases, there is little financial incentive—and in the latter case, sometimes companies charge to dispose of battery "cores"—that probably limit the program's effectiveness. Asking people to remove the burned-out bulbs, store them, and then remember to take them on their next trip to the store is less convenient than simply throwing them out in the regular trash collection (as bad as that is for the environment).

Often, when there is no visible "return," companies can do little more than "suggest" the way in which their products are used and ultimately disposed of (or recycled). Manufacturers of computers, cell phones, and a host of electronic devices offer power- (and energy-) saving tips for consumers, but over 90 percent of the electricity used today for computers is not used in the "server" room but at individual desktop stations that are left on at night and monitors that are left on when laptops are disconnected. In homes, chargers that live their lives in the outlet are drawing power even when the portable device is not attached. TV sets that have not been turned on in weeks are drawing power remembering things like the date and time and the frequency of the last channel viewers watched.

In the 1980s, the Advertising Council attempted to empower people—mostly young people—to "Just Say No" (to Drugs). While the effectiveness of the campaign is questioned today, it is often cited as an example by people seeking to encourage behavior change. In a social situation, when confronted by a friend or trusted peer, it is often hard to avoid succumbing to peer pressure.

Because balancing the issues around climate, health, wellness, societal "good," and "cost" is interrelated, the question is far more complex than a simple Boolean (yes/no) choice. Because these goods often come with a higher price, people may find themselves torn between the immediate needs of their family and the longer-term benefit to the planet or society.

Experts point out that while the percentage of consumers who will pay a premium for "green" products is growing, it remains a small portion of the overall market. As a result, some of the more strident activists are increasingly calling for the elimination of certain products that do not meet their criteria for environmental or social standards. Get rid of the "bad," their argument goes, and consumers will have no choice but to purchase "superior" products. But as we saw with prohibition, outright banning of a product (or class of products) for which there is a strong market does not force societal change; it creates a "black" market that often gives rise to other social ills, such as the rise of organized crime.

Companies would do well to recognize that in a competitive marketplace, any company that makes the decision to eliminate products and services that its customers demand is likely to find itself sacrificing customers and risking market share potentially to disastrous financial effect. That is why sustainability efforts that are true to the concept of people-planet-prosperity and building a virtuous cycle seek to find ways to promote conscious consumerism.

According to the latest research from the Shelton Group, the leading marketing and communications firm that focuses exclusively on sustainability and conducts regular research to keep ahead of ever-changing attitudes and behaviors, 42 percent of Americans want to be *seen* as someone who buys green products. Suzanne Shelton, founder and CEO, explains: "It is now a matter of personal image, and how people want to be viewed by their family, friends and colleagues."

This represents a fundamental shift, because sustainable products are not part of peoples' self-image. Therefore, the opportunity exists for companies to create and sell things that are visibly "green."

For example, of the 20 percent of Americans who say that they are in the market for a new home in the next few years, more than half (55 percent) prioritize things like energy efficiency and sustainability. But while homebuilders may focus on things like "tighter" buildings and more insulation to save energy, buyers are looking for visible expressions such as solar panels, high-efficiency EnergyStar appliances, and "smart" thermostats and appliances. Things like high-efficiency heating and cooling systems, while having a larger energy impact, are less important to purchasers. "Consumers value what (people) can see because it says something about them," explains Shelton.

This represents a shift in how people are thinking. And this attitude is driving actual purchasing decisions.

Today, a quarter of Americans can provide the name of a manufacturer that they have purchased from (or chose not to purchase from) based on environmental attributes. That is up from 6 percent only a few years ago.

The gap between the 42 percent who want to be perceived as environmentally responsible purchasers and the 25 percent who actually are may seem daunting. But Shelton points out, intention is always ahead of action. She encourages, "As that 42 percent increases, we will see the percentage who can actually name an example will grow too."

Consumers today are blessed with many choices, but because people increasingly want to be viewed as being on the right side of the environmental issue, companies can gain market advantage by sending the visual cues—like EnergyStar labels or other environmentally or socially responsible labels. A prime example is electric cars, like the BMW i3 and Toyota Prius, that offer radically different and recognizable designs so that they are unmistakably electric vehicles.

Unilever has made a study of encouraging sustainable living. The have identified five "levers" that drive behavior change by overcoming barriers, enabling triggers, and leading to motivation (Figure 4.2).[8]

This winning formula helped form the basis behind Sodexo's successful WasteLESS Week, a program that sought to make reducing waste use easy, desirable, fun, and rewarding. People were encouraged to share pledges that they were making, actions that they were taking, and results that they were achieving using a variety of social media platforms. This extended the effort across cities, regions, and countries in friendly competition to see who could have the most fun and make the greatest difference. Within a week results could be seen, measured, and compared. That provided the reward—much like declining numbers on a scale (or increasing grades) serve as positive reinforcement. Even the counter showing the number of water bottles saved on a water dispenser provides positive reinforcement. As a college student explained, "if the person before

---

[8]Unilever. 2011. "Inspiring Sustainable Living: Expert Insights into Consumer Behavior and Unilever's Five Levers for Change." https://www.unilever.com/Images/slp_5-levers-for-change_tcm244-414399_en.pdf.

Figure 4.2 Old habits are hard to change, but by making it easy, fun, desirable, and rewarding, people can be motivated to change their ways without shame, guilt, or punishment

me didn't trigger it to add a bottle, I can get it to go up two, when I fill my 12-oz. reusable container."

A word of caution about the concept of "fun." Sustainability is often seen as an outlier or "nice to do" and less an integral strategy for the business. Making it fun should not cross the line into making it frivolous or seem childish. Events and messages that are compellingly memorable and spark the imagination while still demonstrating their strategic value and importance is the goal.

This supports a more reasoned and reasonable approach, using one's expertise to make the healthier, socially responsible, environmental choices compelling to customers. Customers who trust you will be receptive to messages that offer information (rather than condemnation) about the impacts associated with different products. This is an example of using "Expertise" in the "Actions–Influence–Expertise" framework because the company is empowering them to make choices for themselves that match their values—even as their values may shift over time and as economic circumstances may vary—rather than removing choices or attempting to guilt/shame people into compliance.

People often find themselves choosing between powerful value drivers such as early economy cars that offered terrible reliability, questionable safety, marginal comfort, and poor performance in exchange for better gas mileage. While higher prices at the pump may be the primary reason for increasing sales in this segment, the fact that today these cars manage to combine fuel efficiency with other desirable features such as power, performance, 5-star safety ratings, navigation systems, keyless entry, Bluetooth, etc., is certainly part of their increasing popularity.

In the end, success will not be defined simply by making sustainable product available, but by the percentage of your sales they encompass. Somewhere between the 25 and 42 percent identified by Suzanne Shelton is the "sweet spot." And then, by using your expertise to make the products superior in the eyes of customers, you can work to increase the proportion.

A powerful example of a program that fulfills all three—actions, influence, and expertise—is the efforts of the Sodexo Group to reduce food waste, based on its primary and historic business as an institutional food service provider for thousands of schools (from grade schools to colleges and universities), hospitals, businesses, and senior living facilities.

Today, an estimated one-third of the food produced in the world goes to waste. That is equal to about 1.3 billion tons of fruits, vegetables, meat, dairy, seafood, and grains that never leave the farm, get lost or spoiled during distribution, or are thrown away in hotels, grocery stores, restaurants, schools, or home kitchens. It could be enough calories to feed every undernourished person on the planet.

Reducing food waste is not only a financial imperative for the company, it also can help end hunger around the world (by redirecting food that would not be eaten to those who need it via food banks and other mechanisms) and reduce climate change—because the use of land to produce food has major impacts, as does decomposing food in the fields, during transportation and in landfills.

But wasted food is not just a social or humanitarian concern—it is an environmental one as well. When we waste food, we also waste all the energy and water it takes to grow, harvest, transport, and package it. And if food goes to the landfill and rots, it produces methane—a greenhouse gas even more potent than CO_2. About 11 percent of all the greenhouse gas emissions that come from the food system could be reduced if we stop wasting food.

In its own operations, Sodexo has implemented a program called WasteWatch powered by Leanpath. In-kitchen trackers weigh and identify food that is not consumed. The data are automatically analyzed, providing detailed information showing what is being wasted and why. The program cuts food waste an average of 50 percent, with some units achieving even higher rates of savings. Sam Smith, director of marketing for Leanpath shares: "All of our tools and support are focused on behavior change: giving kitchens the tools, data and support to make smart decisions and change the behaviors of their staff that lead to food waste."[9] Managers, who are responsible for the profitability of their units can clearly see the savings.

At the same time, the company engaged in efforts to encourage its clients (the facilities) and consumers to "take only what you intend to eat" during its annual WasteLESS Week. A combination of engagement activities, including filling a clear Lucite column with the bread left on cafeteria trays each day, increased awareness, did not shame individuals, and demonstrated the cumulative impact of individual action. Every time this visual was used the amount of bread left uneaten was substantially reduced.

Company chefs also prepared free tastings of innovative food items made from things like stale bread or overripe bananas. And while croutons and banana bread (for example) are familiar to many, they also took advantage of the company's global reach, using recipes from around the world that used atypical parts of fruits and vegetables to introduce exotic tastes such as a Brazilian recipe for broccoli soup. The culmination of these events was a free downloadable WasteLESS recipe collection of the more popular items including a way to make beer or ale from stale bread

---

[9]S. Smith. 2019. Correspondence with the author for this publication.

(Belgium), an authentic Lancashire Hot Pot from the UK, and pear and chocolate pudding from France.

The company also reaches back to its supply chain, using its purchasing partners to leverage opportunities for unattractive, and therefore unmarketable, fruits and vegetables to be used for recipes (such as pies or soups) where the nutritional value can be used. The company also spearheaded the creation of a not-for-profit International Food Waste Coalition that brought the effort full circle with a student engagement campaign, teaching young children the true value of food based on the concept that people do not waste something that they consider valuable.

It is important to note that while it may seem intuitive that managing one's own actions is the simplest or easiest thing to do, that is not always the case, particularly in a large and decentralized organization like a multinational company. In the case of Sodexo, the WasteLESS Week promotional campaign grew faster and gained more traction. Its popularity with the company's clients (and customers) may have helped encourage local managers to invest more time and money in implementing WasteWatch in their own kitchens, after seeing the popularity and measuring the impact that the waste reduction campaign had with consumers (Figures 4.3).

Other examples of companies that are working across their value chains to engage their suppliers as well as customers include UK clothing retailer Marks & Spencer that, in addition to its supplier standards, also encourages shoppers to bring their unwanted garments back to any of M&S stores in the UK and leave them in recycling bins by the checkout in a program called "Shwopping" (a contraction of shopping and swapping).

Discussion Questions

1. Map your current efforts against this framework.

2. What "gaps" can you identify?

3. How will you fill them?

Influence			Actions				Expertise			
How our values are integrated into business decisions			How we demonstrate our values through our business				How we encourage others to adopt			
• Brand promise – our values guide with whom we do business • Be the benchmark for excellence			• Our culture as differentiator • Brand promise – to maintain the highest standards • Be the benchmark for Operational Excellence				• Leverage the strength of our people • Brand promise – helping others live their values			
Business practices (labor, diversity & inclusion, etc.)	Business Sector / Industry	Supply chain	Promise	Plan	Program	Performance	Drive client actions	Encourage customer decisions	Increase public awareness/ expectations	Facilitate behavior change
			Aspirational Commitments	• Goals • Timelines • Milestones	• Initiatives • Programs • Efforts	• Measurement • Public Reporting • Third party validations				
International Food Waste Coalition			• Operations in all countries where Sodexo operates will deliver on US Sustainable Development Goal 12.3 – halve food waste by consumers by 2030 and reduce in value chain	• Implement program at 3,000 sites worldwide within a year	• WasteWatch by Leanpath	• Percent of sites participating • Percentage food waste reduced (aggregate) • Percent food waste reduced (by country) • Percent food waste reduced (by location)	• WasteLESS Week engagement campaign • Food waste cook book			

Figure 4.3 A real-world example of how a commitment to reduce food waste resulted in programs for both suppliers and clients/customers. The engagement campaign included posters, stickers, and interactive activities, including Augmented Reality, that triggered a video when people pointed their mobile devices at the posters.

	Influence How our values are integrated into business decisions		Actions How we demonstrate our values through our business				Expertise How we encourage others to adopt			
	• Brand promise – our values guide with whom we do business • Be the benchmark for excellence		• Our culture as differentiator • Brand promise – to maintain the highest standards • Be the benchmark for Operational Excellence				• Leverage the strength of our people • Brand promise – helping others live their values			
	↓	↓	Promise	Plan	Program	Performance	↑	↑	↑	↑
	Business Sector / Industry	Supply chain	Aspirational Commitments	• Goals • Timelines • Milestones	• Initiatives • Programs • Efforts	• Measure-ment • Public Reporting • Third party validations	Drive client actions	Encourage customer decisions	Increase public awareness/ expectations	Facilitate behavior change
Business practices (labor, diversity & inclusion, etc.)										
Environment										
Social										
Governance										

Figure 4.4 Worksheet for evaluating or developing sustainability programs. This can help identify gaps (for planning) as well as helping to illustrate, as was done in Figure 4.3, how to demonstrate the comprehensive nature of an effort

CHAPTER 5

How Sustainability Is Changing Traditional Functions of Business

Sustainability has quantifiable impacts on the general public's willingness to buy from, invest in, and work for a given company—all things that directly impact corporate success.

The Reputation Institute relies on data to make the case. Their 2018 Global CR RepTrak 100 global survey, which is based on more than 230,000 ratings, found:

> Globally, corporate social responsibility (CSR) drives 40 percent of corporate reputation. Companies that excel in CSR receive massive levels of support, with over 90 percent of the general public willing to purchase their products or over 80 percent willing to give the company the benefit-of-the-doubt in a time of corporate crisis.[1]

The bottom line for businesses is that companies with an excellent reputation perform better and are insulated against failure.

The Power of Purpose—What You Make Is Not What You Do

Public interest in corporate responsibility is unusually high: The September 2019 issue of *Fortune* article "A New Purpose for the Corporation"

---

[1]Reputation Institute. 2018. "Corporate Social Responsibility—Align Perception with Reality." https://insights.reputationinstitute.com/blog-ri/corporate-social-responsibility-align-perception-with-reality, (accessed October 5, 2019).

featured the results of a survey that found that nearly three-quarters (72 percent) of American adults agree that public companies should be "mission driven" as well as focused on shareholders and customers. The research found that many Americans (64 percent) say that a company's "primary purpose" should include "making the world better" and many also say it should include "making money for shareholders."

The power of purpose comes through talking to people like Henk Campher, vice president of corporate marketing and head of #giveahoot for Hootsuite. Henk remembers when sustainability started out, more than 20 years ago, with the model of minimizing negative impacts (do less harm). By contrast, "At Salesforce from day one it has been all about how the company can maximize the positive impacts."

He quotes the CEO, Marc Benioff: "The Business of Business is to Improve the State of the World."

It's a pretty unique setup. How does a B2B CRM company beat Tesla as the most innovative company? They do it by allowing employees to completely be themselves. If you're distracted by not being you, you can't be brave and innovative.

Describing the well-known situation several years ago, when the head of HR confronted the CEO with the fact that the organization did not offer pay parity for men and women, his response was incredulous, but he didn't deny it. He asked for the data, stating "if it is true, bring me the data so we can fix it." When it was revealed that it would cost $3,000,000 to bring the company back in line, "Nobody blinked. It's just what they needed to do." Henk explains that because of its growth by acquisition, the company has had to check every year to make sure that they're still living their values.

According to the chief ethical use officer "That's the culture. It's open to challenge. It makes it difficult sometimes. Sometimes there's no answer because no one else has done it. We set up an office for ethical use. How do we know our products are improving the state of the world?"

For Henk the challenges that he sees, and the progress he has seen made, continue to ignite his passion, even after 20 years working in sustainability:

This isn't about advancing myself, it is about being part of something that's advancing the world. I cannot live in a world where a kid dies every 3 seconds from a preventable disease, or where climate change is going to choke our future. But I can live in a world where I am working to help fix those things. I've managed to marry my passion for changing the world and my skill at story-telling. I was just lucky to be able to marry those two.[2]

As with the discussion in Chapter 1, we can quantify *the business benefits* of being a purpose-driven organization.

Attracting, Hiring, Retaining, and Engaging Employees

57 percent of the general public are willing to work for a company with an excellent reputation—Reputation Institute, 2018[3]

Typically, baby boomers favored workplaces that offered stability and high pay. Research shows that new, younger workers entering the workforce today want something different. Millennials will make up 75 percent of the workforce by 2025 and they are looking for socially responsible employers. They want purpose and their paycheck to be aligned 100 percent of their time. Cone Communications' Millennial Employee Engagement Study (2016) showed that more than three-quarters (76 percent) are using corporate values as a screen when they seek employment.[4]

Writing in Talent Economy, Peggi Pelosi explains:

For businesses that want to stay competitive in the hiring market, the first thing to know is that millennials are not looking for the

---

[2]H. Campher. September 12, 2019. Interview with the author.

[3]Reputation Institute. 2018. "Companies with an Excellent Reputation Perform Better and Are Insulated Against Failure." https://www.reputationinstitute.com/solutions, (accessed October 5, 2019).

[4]Cone Communications. 2016. "Millennial Employee Engagement Study." https://static1.squarespace.com/static/56b4a7472b8dde3df5b7013f/t/5819e8b303596e301 6ca0d9c/1478092981243/2016+Cone+Communications+Millennial+Employee+En gagement+Study_Press+Release+and+Fact+Sheet.pdf

same things from their employers that the boomers were. That means your organization will have to evolve and innovate in order to stay relevant, attract quality employees and retain top performers in the new millennial marketplace.[5]

The Cone study also found that:

- 75 percent of millennials would take a job for a *lower salary* if it meant working for a socially responsible company.
- 64 percent of millennials say that they will not take a job if a potential employer does not have strong corporate responsibility practices.

A company makes certain products and/or services. They may be diversified or specialized, but they also need to remember that what they *make* is not the same as what they *do*. The products and services themselves have no intrinsic value; their value lies in their impact of peoples' lives—both intended and unintended. Like the classic example of the three masons (see box), it is important to help employees to remember why what they are doing matters to people every day. The value that they bring to their task is far more than the ability to bring home a paycheck. Knowing how what you make impacts peoples' lives is the core of defining your corporate responsibility—knowing how people who use your goods or services benefit from your products and maximizing that positive impact.

It is hard for anyone to get truly excited about the number of linear feet of wallboard being produced or the tons of aggregates being crushed, but when the focus shifts to how those things are used in real life it become more inspiring for any worker when the company mission is linked to the fact that they

are building the homes where we will raise our children, the hospitals where they will be born, the schools where they will be

---

[5] P. Pelosi. 2019. "Millennials Want Workplaces with Social Purpose. How Does Your Company Measure Up?" https://www.chieflearningofficer.com/2018/02/20/millennials-want-workplaces-social-purpose-company-measure/, (accessed August 9, 2019).

educated, the offices where they will work, the houses of worship where they may one day get married and start a family of their own … and the roads that they'll use to get to those places.

Suddenly the mission of the organization becomes more than production figures—it becomes "Materials for Building Our World," which became Lafarge's company tagline for several years.

Social purpose organizations are not immune from losing sight of the bigger picture. The National Committee for Quality Assurance (NCQA)

The Three Masons

A man came across three masons who were working at chipping chunks of granite from large blocks. The first seemed unhappy at his job, chipping away and frequently looking at his watch. When the man asked what he was doing, the first mason responded: "I'm hammering this rock."

The second mason, seemingly more interested in his work, was hammering diligently and when asked what it was that he was doing, answered, "I'm molding this block of rock so that it can be used to construct a wall."

The third mason was working carefully, taking time to stand back and evaluate his work. He chipped off small pieces until he was satisfied that it was the best he could do. When he was questioned about his work he proudly stated, "I am building a cathedral!"

owns and administers the Healthcare Effectiveness Data and Information Set (HEDIS). A total of 190 million people are enrolled in plans that report HEDIS results. The organization's mission was summed up as "measuring the quality of healthcare." Not only was this hardly unique (many other organizations made the same claim) it was also only an accurate summation of what the organization made; an annual report showed how more and more plans were adopting more and more services to score higher on their rankings (that were published annually in *U.S. News & World Report*).

The "bigger" picture was an increasing number of health plans offering an increasing number of services that were linked to improved health outcomes. Applying this principle, the organization adopted a new tagline "measuring quality, improving health care," which more accurately captures the impact of what the organization does for the lives of 190 million people. This remains the organization's tagline more than a decade after the change was first suggested.

Sometimes a direct linkage to the sustainability program can be made. For Lafarge, the tagline "Materials for Building our World" inspired "Building a Better World." For Sodexo "Making Every Day a Better Day" begat the "Better Tomorrow Plan" (which initially was in a speech: "if we are truly making every day a better day then we are also making every tomorrow a better tomorrow"). In this way, the sustainability program became an outgrowth of the social purpose of the organization and helped drive that social purpose home to prospective employees as well as existing employees, communities, and, of course, customers.

Campher touches on this benefit as well: "One of the reasons we do it, is people. In a highly competitive market, how do you get the best minds? You attract them because we appeal to their values."

It is important to engage employees based on what is important to them. The Washington DC region is notorious for its traffic congestion. The 2016 State of the Commute Survey conducted by the Metropolitan Washington Council of Governments (MWCOG) found that 43 percent of survey respondents reported changing jobs or residence due to their commutes, and 63 percent made commuting the only factor considered in their decision whether to accept a job.[6]

WGL, a Washington DC-based energy company, allows employees to work from home 1, 2, or 3 days per week (depending on their role, job requirements, etc.) as part of their "Reduce the Commute" program. The program was recognized by the Washington DC District Department of Transportation with the 2019 Telework Employer Ambassador Award from goDCgo for the company's data-driven telework program.[7] After

---

[6]MWCOG. 2016. "Commuter Connections: State of the Commute Survey." https://www.mwcog.org/assets/1/28/Item__5_-_2016_SOC_Draft_Technical_Report_092016.pdf, (accessed September 12, 2019).

[7]goDCgo. 2019. "Employer Ambassador Awards." http://info.godcgo.com/ambassadorawardswinners, (accessed August 22, 2019).

many years of reporting miles avoided (not traveled) and the associated cost (for gasoline) and environmental savings (CO_2e),* participation in the program had stagnated. It was rejuvenated by adding two questions to the employee survey: (1) How much time do you save? and (2) How important is this program to you?

The results demonstrated that, thanks to the local congestion, the average employee who worked from home once a week saved the equivalent of more than a week and a half of extra annual leave (vacation). The second question revealed that employees who participated value the program above 9 on a scale of 1 to 10. Surprisingly, the importance did not correlate to distance of commute or to the gender of the employee. The Talent Acquisition Team added that fact to their conversations with all prospective employees (to help attract, hire, and retain employees) so the sustainability effort that (also) has prevented 57,000 trips, avoided driving 1,560,000 miles, and saved more than 70,000 gallons of fuel and avoided 618 CO_2e since 2010 is also helping make the company a more attractive employer.

Michel Landel, CEO of the Sodexo Group, described that organization's commitment to improving the quality of life of its employees as a driver of both customer and shareholder satisfaction in "The Myth of Shareholder Value" in Forbes in 2015:

> It's not a sustainable model ... for a company to serve its customers, it needs to engage its people, not destroy labor. Companies have a role in society. We can't ignore the world we live in. We have to make sure employees have a decent life.[8]

That sense of accountability to employees is not unique. While most corporate structures are built like a pyramid, narrowing down to the "top" management, Ted Balfe, president and CEO of Lafarge Construction

---

*CO_2e reductions from WGL's telework program were not included or claimed as part of the company's overall greenhouse gas emissions reductions results as they were outside the company's operational control (Scope 3).

[8] P. Dwyer. 2015. "The Myth of Shareholder Value," *Bloomberg*. https://www .bloomberg.com/opinion/articles/2015-05-11/shareholder-value-isn-t-the-only-way-to-run-a-successful-company, (accessed August 28, 2019).

Materials, was known for physically turning the organization chart upside-down to illustrate that the fate of more than a thousand employees (and their families) rested on the decisions of a few people. "Make a mistake, and you may be gone," he would say. "But if I make a mistake, hundreds of people, and their families, pay the price." Far from arrogance, he was saying this to reinforce the sense of responsibility and accountability he felt for the people who had placed their trust in him and his leadership team.

All corporate leaders ought to have this awareness reinforced occasionally and, better yet, to extend it beyond their employees, customers, and shareholders to include all their stakeholders. For example, applying the same thinking to relationships with suppliers (through giving them business and sharing best practices) a company has access to better supplies and materials from which to make its products or deliver its services. Engaging in environmentally damaging practices can impact the health and well-being of everyone in the community and, in the case of climate change, the entire world.

Bertrand Collomb understood this well and put it succinctly:

Trust for any economic player will be based on the perception that it is useful for society, that its economic success is a plus for the common good, and that its success can be achieved without abusing people, inside and outside the organization, and without being unethical.[9]

Discussion Questions

1. Apply the concept "what you make is not what you do" to a sample business or organization. How does their current messaging align with this?

2. How would you improve their messaging to be more purpose-based?

3. Can you apply the same principle to yourself? What impact are you—or do you hope—to make? On whom?

---

[9] S. Rangan. October, 2015. *Performance and Progress: Essays on Capitalism, Business, and Society* (Oxford, UK: Oxford University Press, p. 471). https://www.amazon .com/Performance-Progress-Capitalism-Business-Society/dp/0198744285.

Earning Passionate Customers

Each time they make a purchasing decision customers choose to support or punish a set of established economic, political, social, and faith paradigms. While some people find themselves limited in their choices due to economic necessity or geography, many have the power to choose. Ultimately consumers must face the decision—are they willing to pay more, travel further, or even do without something in order to reward companies (and systems) that share our values or do they turn a blind eye and remain passively complicit?

Increasingly customers are aware that every time they spend money, they are effectively casting a vote for the kind of world they want. Shelton Group's research into consumer attitudes and behaviors applies here as well. "Consumers want to buy from companies that have environmental and social purpose. They see these things as inter-related, just as the sustainable development goals do," says Shelton.[10] Corporate structures may separate social and environmental efforts, but she points out that "that's the way everyone is looking at it, other than corporate America, that it is all one."

This points out that the very nature of sustainability is to link social, environmental, and governance issues together, whereas corporate structures tend to compartmentalize them. Customers who view the company do not care where or how those things are managed, as long as they are managed and managed well.

In 2018 Shelton Group released the results of the research in *Social Purpose Is the New Black*. They found:

Consumers believe companies should take a stand—and they'll support that stand with their purchases; 64 percent of those who said it is "extremely important" for a company to take a stand on a social issue said they were "very likely" to purchase a product based on that commitment.

- Hellmann's mayonnaise supports the production of cage-free eggs, a key ingredient in its product.
- The TOMS One for One program matches each pair of shoes bought with the donation of shoes to a child in need.

---

[10] S. Shelton. August 7, 2019. Interview by the author.

- Stella Artois has been supporting clean drinking water for people in the developing world since 2015 and asking consumers to "Buy a Lady a Drink" through their chalice purchase promotion.

Shelton explains the importance of linking to causes that make sense from a business standpoint:

> These companies started with their core business and identified a social purpose that made sense for them. This doesn't mean companies can't or shouldn't get involved in a variety of causes, but it's much more likely consumers will remember your brand's cause if it relates to your primary product or service. So, that's where you should focus your storytelling and marketing efforts.

Other examples of strategic giving that link back to the organization's core mission are Lafarge's partnership with Habitat for Humanity International and Sodexo's creation of its own STOP Hunger not-for-profit and International Food Waste Coalition. No one will question a construction materials company donating construction materials (and labor) to help build homes for those in the community, nor a food service company understanding the importance and value of having enough to eat.

In fact, in the Shelton study, more than half of the people who could name a brand that had improved in their minds because of a social stand it had taken said it was because the brand "took a stand on an issue that aligns with products and services they offer." Slightly *fewer* recalled brands that supported one of the respondent's personal favorite causes.[11] This seems to indicate that the connection between the cause and the core business is the strongest when the cause and the business purpose are seen as a natural alignment.

Out of 30 percent of those who named a brand that had improved in their minds because of the social stand it took,

---

[11]Shelton Group. 2018. "Social Purpose Is the New Black." https://storage.googleapis.com/shelton-group/Pulse%20Reports/Brands%20%26%20Stands%20-%20Final%20Report%202018.pdf, (accessed August 12, 2019).

- 16 percent said it was because the brand "took a stand on an issue that aligns with products and services they offer."
- 13 percent said it was because they "found out they support one of my favorite causes."
- 11 percent said it was because the brand "took a stand on a current social issue."

Shelton further explained that "the most meaningful stances are those that make the deliberate decision to walk away from money for a purpose, whether it is environmental or social." Examples of this include CVS walking away from $2 billion in revenue by refusing to sell cigarettes, companies that forgo participation in "Black Friday" sales events, and Chick-fil-A's policy to close on Sundays.

Of this actions, perhaps nothing represents aligning and rebranding with social purpose more than CVS' decision. Not only did the company stop selling tobacco products, it rebranded itself as CVS Health. Beyond the initial public relations and social media frenzy, the company was rewarded with higher sales and stock price. Those trends have continued, according to *Cigarettes Out. Health In. An analysis of the rebrand of CVS Health*, a 2015 Arthur W. Page Society Case Study.[12]

This is not surprising, as we saw earlier in the Monks and Lajoux research (see section "Attracting Investment Capital" in Chapter 2), corporate reputation is an integral driver of shareholder value. While shareholders may have initially been concerned about the lost revenue, customers rewarded the company standing behind its values and, thus, revenues did not suffer. In this way, taking a stand on a social value that links to the business helps to reduce risk.

In July 2019 *Forbes* reported on a study that offered similar results and insights.[13] Accenture found that a brand's purpose, and the trust that accompanies it, influences purchasing decisions. They're basing those

[12]CVS Health. 2015. "Cigarettes Out. Health In. An analysis of the rebrand of CVS Health." https://communication.depaul.edu/about/news-and-events/2015/Documents/ArthurPageSocietyAwards15/PageCVSStudy15.pdf, (accessed August 12, 2019).
[13]J. Fromm. 2019." Brands Still Matter, If They're Fueled by Purpose." https://www.forbes.com/sites/jefffromm/2019/07/11/brands-still-matter-if-theyre-fueled-by-purpose/#3486eeba3b0a, (accessed August 12, 2019).

decisions on how brands operate in the real world. The article quotes Ivan Pollard, chief marketing officer at General Mills. "Numerous studies demonstrate over 60 percent of Millennials say, for example, that 'it is essential that a brand shares and promotes the values I care about.'" But, he cautions, it is not about marketing or messaging:

> In today's world, a brand telling its consumers its purpose is not very effective. With the pervasive transparency of today, to win a consumer's trust a brand should be what it says it is, do what it believes it should and only then will other people say what its purpose might be.

Purpose is the driver of authenticity and trust. Without a meaningful purpose, brands will struggle for relevancy and, thereby, lose opportunities for increased share in an ever more competitive environment.

Investors That Are True Stakeholders

Short-term investors are more interested in making money, and less in the long-term viability of the company. In many ways, they mark a distinction between shareholders and stakeholders. If they are not investing over the long term (as employees, customers, suppliers, and communities are) then it is fair to say that they are not stakeholders at all. Companies should then do well by focusing on those who "buy and hold" as well as the other stakeholder groups mentioned above.

Indeed, the long term investment strategy in companies one believes in has long been the model espoused by Warren Buffett, one of the most successful investors of all time. The focus on maximizing short-term (i.e., quarterly) returns tends to create "bubbles" as we have seen in everything from tulip bulbs in the 1600's to the housing market in the early 2000's (where flippers bought/updated/sold in record numbers) followed by crashes. Increasingly investors are again recognizing the wisdom of taking the longer view, based on the stark lessons of the Great Recession of 2008.

The Long-Term Approach: Building a Legacy

What would inspire a 176-year-old whisky maker to launch a project and to sponsor a 3-day meeting of marine biologists from around the world dedicated to the preservation and cultivation of the Native European Flat Oyster?

Louise Schiavone, journalist and senior lecturer at Johns Hopkins University Carey Business School in Washington, DC and Baltimore, Maryland, caught up with Peter Nelson, operations director for the Glenmorangie Company (part of the wine and spirits group of LVMH Moët Hennessy Louis Vuitton S.A.), at the 3-day Native Oyster Restoration Alliance conference in Edinburgh, Scotland. He told a conference of professionals from government, science, business, and academia:

quite bluntly, we decided that water and the ocean are a really good thing for us. We want to do things outside of making whisky that improve our reputation or improve our sustainability. Number one thing is profit: you have to make money.

She went on to interview Dan Laffoley, principal advisor on marine science and conservation for the Global Marine and Polar Program for the Switzerland-based International Union for Conservation of Nature (IUCN),

If you look at certain parts of the drinks sector, they invest in a different way against time. Glenmorangie invests over a considerable period of time because that's how long it takes to make the product. Their customer base is faithful to them. They buy the latest special releases. So, you've got a very time-based commitment which matches well with trying to do what they're doing with oyster reefs.

The point of the Glenmorangie story, Laffoley told Schiavone, is this:

You can talk the talk. And we see the FTSE 100 has the "Green Awards," which I'm sure has considerable value as a beacon for what industry should be doing. But in the middle of this you actually want to have real things happening in real places. That's what's exciting about the Glenmorangie model: the fact that you do have real things happening in real places that are groundbreaking.[14]

---

[14]L. Schiavone. September 13, 2019. "The Time Has Come to Talk About Oysters," *LA Review of Books.* https://lareviewofbooks.org/article/the-time-has-come-to-talk-about-oysters/

Indeed, The Glenmorangie Company is doing something no other whisky company is doing in Scotland. Its inception, to be clear, was motivated by the need to comply with the changing landscape of environmental regulations and, also, to appeal to emerging green-minded younger consumers to give them the final incentives, as it were, to spend a little extra on premium Scotch whisky. "When I talk about sustainability, I'm not really talking about the planet or what's to become of it," said Nelson at the conference. "We need to be sustainable because we believe we'll be making more whisky into the future, providing employment, providing pleasure to people, and creating profit."

Note how this incorporates the idea of "what you make is not what you do"—the focus is not on increasing the number of bottles or barrels but rather on pleasure (presumably from the whisky itself) and also employment opportunities as well as generating a profit for the owners.

Discussion Questions

1. Have the values of an organization influenced your decision to purchase or not?

2. Do you look for responsible products or is it the overall company that matters more?

3. How should management "test" their stands with their own employee base? Should they? What should they do if a percentage of their employees disagree with the company stand?

From Storytelling to Engagement

The role of communications department has dramatically and irrevocably changed in recent years. The instant-information age has not only changed the ways in which information is shared, it has exponentially increased the amount of information that people both need and receive. In media relations, the news cycle has expanded to 24 hours; and the increasing prevalence and importance of nontraditional social media (and the increasing influence of bloggers and citizen-journalists) have required more than a change in tactics.

These changes in the world around us have fundamentally changed—increased—stakeholder expectations and, as a result, traditional communications functions are being redefined as well. Organizations that wish to communicate with credibility are moving from "spin" and toward "transparency," inviting and hosting the conversation that increasingly must be more open about their aspirations and their efforts to achieve them—sometimes even acknowledging their shortcomings. In this way, companies shift their focus to actions and a higher degree of transparency with stakeholders than ever before.

This is why the connection between sustainability programs and corporate communications efforts is more than a philosophical one. Because of the strong and increasing importance that employees, customers, clients, and communities place on the environmental, social, and economic impacts an organization has, many of the duties traditionally assigned to a company's communications department to build internal buy-in (organizational culture and employee engagement) and reputational capital (external, community, and public relations) can best be accomplished by maximizing the effective development, implementation, management, and communication of sustainability efforts across a company.

Companies often focus on telling "their story" and wanting people to know it. "We want to be a loved brand" is the charge that marketers and communicators hear every day. If people only understood who we are, the logic goes, they would appreciate us more.

There are some fundamental lessons from the dating world that they need to consider if they want to build a sustainable relationship and not just engage in a series of one-night stands (transactions).

First, like a person, a business cannot, will not, and should not aspire to be loved by everyone.

- Do they want customers to love them for the amazing experience the business gives them?
- Do they want regulators to love their honorable compliance with the rules established for their industry or business?
- Do they want your suppliers to love them for their generous and flexible terms and conditions?

What happens when doing one directly conflicts with another and the business must choose? For example, if suppliers are unable to provide what is needed to give the customer that "amazing" experience?

In short, trying too hard to be loved by everyone will earn you the respect of no one.

Another lesson is that if you want to be loved, you need to love yourself first.

The key to passionate customer loyalty often lies with employees. Make sure that they love the business and its values and put that into visible expression every day in front of every customer. Make that your story.

A long-term relationship requires commitment. People need to fall in love with enduring attributes, not the temporary or illusory.

Communications departments that are tasked with putting a good face on things in order to get people to love your brand, marketers or business development people who promise the stars and the moon (without worrying about whether the business can deliver on its promises) are trying to make people fall in love with who you wish you were, or who you want to be. That's not the same thing as who you are.

The last thing, and perhaps the most important of all, is to really focus on having a relationship with them. This is where storytelling can only go so far. Just like a date with a new interest or a long-term partner, each interaction is comprised of give-and-take, of sharing ideas, and not simply telling the other about their day.

Storytelling is a common brand engagement strategy because, when done well, it connects users to an organization emotionally.

The "invitation to a conversation" strategy drives engagement to a distinctly higher level.

That is why some companies are shifting from telling "their story" to the real value of using their story as an invitation to a conversation. Increasingly people are not interested in just hearing (or reading) a company story, they want to interact. When they post on a company page (or website like Yelp), tweet or (even) write a letter, they *expect* a real response, not a form letter. They want and expect their concerns to be addressed.

Asbury Senior Living retirement community understands that people have strong perceptions about retirement communities and that baby boomers, in particular, more often are "aging in place" and only seeking a community when they need care. People are often reluctant to leave the homes that they have known and move somewhere that they associate with the skilled nursing care and institutional settings where they may have seen their parents spend their final years.

In 2011 Asbury launched a promotional campaign for their HealthAbility program featuring senior residents snow tubing, competing in the Senior Olympics, and even skydiving. The idea, recalls Mike Solomon, a VP of Marketing who has spent years creating experiential brands, was more than simply telling their story:

> The campaign was really ahead of its time because, by showing seniors living their best lives, were able to start conversations about aging and retirement living. Rather than seeing it as a showcase for what we offered, people responded by opening up and telling us their "bucket lists" of what they always wanted to do.

"By voluntarily contributing their wants and dreams through a personal story, customers were actually inserting themselves into Asbury's brand promise. The upside benefit to Asbury is its customers were helping to define the its brand, keeping it rich and continually relevant," explains Solomon.[15]

In the case of digital media, unlike people who tend to act more politely in public, the knowledge that the conversation is taking place where others are privy to what is being said—by both parties—often makes it more uncomfortable for the business. That is why many will respond with a request to "reach out to us directly" and sharing their contact information.

Other companies will answer complaints and questions in the public forum, recognizing and appreciating that those online, public interactions are part of a business story; and can actually help define a business.

Fast food company Wendy's is known for engaging and doing so with a bit of humor (but never at customers' expense). When two other companies engaged in a friendly banter about who was selling more over a particular holiday weekend, Wendy's chimed in asking why they were arguing which

---

[15]M. Solomon. 2019. Correspondence with the author.

of them was the "second best" sandwich. It was clever, a bit cheeky, and showed that the company has a sense of humor. People now tweet @wendys hoping to get a response. At the same time, when a customer does report an issue, they are quick to respond: "Oh no! Please DM us the restaurant location and your phone # so we can make this right. Thanks!"

As a result, the company has a reputation for, almost obviously, being responsive to people.

JetBlue does not just respond to everything, they prioritize responding to tweets where they'd be contributing value. They do not use response rate on Twitter so employees are not pressured to hit a goal by sending quick responses to every single tweet that comes in.

In the blog article "Delighting People in 140 Characters: An Inside Look at JetBlue's Customer Service Success" Laurie Meacham of their digital team is quoted:

> We want our employees to engage smartly, and for the conversations to be organic and natural. We look for opportunities to add value and connect with our customers, not just respond to every single mention that comes our way.[16]

People who witness your interactions also get an impression based on those interactions. And that becomes part of your story. Even a simple interaction, like an overheard conversation, makes an impression.

Twitter User: Hey @JetBlue can I DM a question about upcoming travel?! Thanks!

@JetBlue: Hi! You sure can! What's going on?

Twitter User: Sent you over that DM

@JetBlue: Thanks for following up with us. Give us a few minutes and we'll respond to your DM.

Twitter User: Thanks for being a compassionate and caring airline!
September 4, 2019

---

[16]L. Kolowich. 2014. "Delighting People in 140 Characters: An Inside Look at JetBlue's Customer Service Success," *Hubspot.* https://blog.hubspot.com/marketing/jetblue-customer-service-twitter, (accessed September 4, 2019).

Discussion Questions

1. Does the analogy of building a personal relationship compared to transactional interactions hold true for businesses in your experience?

2. Have you ever felt disappointed by an interaction with a company representative? Was it because they seemed more interested in what they wanted from the interaction than meeting your needs?

3. Are businesses prepared to have "real" conversations? Do they empower their employees to do so?

4. Have you ever been surprised by how a company responded to you (or an interaction you witnessed online)? Was it positive or negative for their reputation?

Thought Leadership to Collaborative Cocreation

The first problem with so many people focusing on "thought leadership" is the myriad of people (and organizations) who confer the title on themselves—rather than understanding that, to be a thought leader, one must be considered such by others.

But the bigger problem with the concept is that it focuses too much on the individual and fails to recognize, appreciate, and encourage the concept of "collaborative cocreation," where more than one person comes together to create something greater than they could have alone.

History is full of examples where great philosophers, artists, and scientists worked together or inspired each other (either collaboratively or competitively): Michelangelo, already a revered master, was challenged anew by the upstart Raphael; and Sir Isaac Newton stated, "If I have seen further it is by standing on the shoulders of Giants."[17]

Eli Whitney did not invent the cotton gin. Versions of it had been around for years. What he did was improve the design, but it is worth noting that others were working on improvements at the same time; and one, John Barclay, was even granted a patent on his slightly different version.

---

[17]https://en.wikiquote.org/wiki/Isaac_Newton.

Alexander Bell was racing against advancements by Thomas Edison when he invented the first working telephone, although Elisha Grey also filed a patent on the same day (he lost his claim in court).

As for Edison, not only did he collaborate—for a time—with Nikola Tesla, he actually in no way invented the incandescent lightbulb. He did find a superior material for the filament, but again that breakthrough was not in isolation.

Gottlieb Daimler and Wilhelm Maybach together designed the first four-wheel automobile with a four-stroke engine, but others, including Benz and Peugeot, were also coming close. Prior to that, several versions (with fewer wheels and different power sources) were already on the scene.

And then there's Orville and Wilbur Wright—the first to fly a heavier-than-air machine. But their efforts started by going back all the way to the drawings of Leonardo DaVinci and built extensively on Otto Liliental's work with gliders. The Wrights deserve credit for what they did—they solved the issue of stability by changing the shape of the wings while turning the rudder (something they observed from birds in flight) — but again, by working together, they were a team.

The point is simply this: The *uber*-focus on individual achievement misses the important point that collaboration and even competition between people often provides the spark and the impetus for transformational change. Today, in the 21st century, we have the unique opportunity afforded by the Internet for like-minded people to work together despite geographic distances, time zone changes, and even languages. While people around the world are trying to come up with great thoughts on their own, there may be someone, half a world away (or across the street) who can offer the missing piece of the puzzle that will turn their idea into a workable solution. Instead of Florence being the nexus for the new Renaissance, it can and likely will be the virtual world.

With issues such as climate change, hunger, poverty, and human rights, do we not owe it to ourselves to work on these issues together?

Discussion Questions

1. Do you prefer to work individually or as a team?

2. Who has inspired you and your thinking?

3. Have you ever had a truly original idea? Was is based on something your heard, read, or saw?

CHAPTER 6

What's Next?

Forces Encouraging Sustainability as a Business Model

Globalization

One hundred years after the first powered flight, the oceans are no longer impenetrable barriers that keep people, ideas, and information apart.

Today people travel more than ever before, and corporations often outsource products and send workers to new locales. This leads to exposure of both companies and individuals to differing practices and societal norms. This invites natural comparisons, with the accompanying pressure for a company to match benefits to the individual and the community that are perceived as beneficial. Companies that wish to relocate employees may find that those employees insist on negotiating for a combination of the "best" benefits from both their "home country" and the "host country." This in turn exposes workers in the host country to the new practices and may put pressure on that office to increase their offering to its local employees. Knowledge of and insistence upon these "best of both worlds" packages puts pressure on the company and indeed business in general that results not only in increased salaries, but also superior benefits such as vacation time, pensions and profit sharing, health insurance, and maternity leave. Sometimes by their very existence in a community a company redefines the local expectations as well—such as by making products that the indigenous population may covet for themselves.

Information Technology

Information is now shared at the speed of a mouse-click. News no longer waits for the morning edition of the paper or the 11 p.m. broadcast. This has fueled an ever-increasing appetite and a growing market for news—as producers, editors, reporters, and writers scramble to fill the increased demand for information created by a 24-hour news cycle. It is important to note that with few exceptions (such as entertainment and show business reporting) nobody ever achieved ratings by filling a serious newscast with "good" or "soft" news.

An obvious example of the power of the Internet to provide swift information around the world is the September 11, 2001 terrorist attacks on New York and Washington, DC. Within 15 minutes of the first plane striking the north tower of the World Trade Center, Web traffic was up by 400 percent at VG Nett. Within an hour, the Internet was literally grinding to a halt, as millions upon millions of people tried to get to the news servers of Sky, BBC, CNN, and other large news providers. This demonstrates how the Internet works in tandem with traditional media: The public may find out about an item of news through another medium (radio, TV, or even word-of-mouth) and then log on to the Internet to get the full picture of the situation. Or vice versa.

Increasing Stakeholder Activism

The concurrent advent of information technology and globalization has combined to increase not only the speed and availability of information, but also a greater ease in the sharing of ideas and values. Together IT and globalization are largely responsible for the rising interest in social responsibility and provide a powerful tool for companies, their stakeholders, and their critics alike to share information. The implication for media relations/public relations professionals cannot be overstated because these changes are not only impacting the mechanisms by and through which information can be shared, but also transforming the content of the messages being disseminated. Most dramatically, the messages must be in alignment with observable actions around the globe.

Companies can no longer expect that information about overseas production facilities and working conditions (such as those at Apple supplier Foxconn) will remain confined to the local area. Likewise, information about beneficial programs that a company or its competitors are using in one part of the world can lead to questions by stakeholders from thousands of miles away. The result is increased scrutiny and a progressively rising bar based on the "best in class" in each industry.

While politicians and scientists debate the facts, the public is becoming increasingly convinced and concerned about the environmental impact of human activity. People see the flooding due to hurricanes, record heat-waves in Europe, satellite images of melting glaciers as connected events based on a changing climate. These stakeholders are looking at the environmental impacts of business with a critical eye.

This increasing stakeholder concern is leading to increasing expectations and demands. A sustainability program in one part of the world may give rise to questions, both from outside and also inside a company, about why a company is not engaging in the practice universally.

Increasing Employee Activism

As a subset of stakeholders, employees deserve special attention. Today, as we have seen, many workers are favoring workplaces that match their personal values. This trend has given rise to this new form of employee activism: not for higher wages or better working conditions for themselves but rather to encourage—or demand—that their employer not profit off of things that they, the employees, do not find appropriate.

Years ago, when a company was planning a lavish annual holiday party they approached a well-known, well-respected, well-liked administrative assistant and asked her to be on the planning committee. Company executives considered this project to be a great opportunity to demonstrate project management skills and be highly visible to the senior executives. Instead, her manager was shocked when she declined the assignment based on the principle that the company should instead be giving the large sum of money in question to help the less fortunate in the community at that time of year. The moral point was heard, and the party was indeed scaled back with the balance of the budget donated to local organizations.

But what happens when management does not listen, or does not believe that enough employees feel that way? Today employees have gotten louder and have gone from individual protests to organized events. Employees at Wayfair, in protest of the company's perfectly legal contract providing products to facilities being used to detain children at the southern U.S. border, walked out and protested the company decision. This was after they sent a letter to senior management asking them to forgo the profits from that specific contract. It is fair to note that it was a minority of employees who signed the letter and protested.

Amazon Employees For Climate Justice, a group of Amazon workers trying to push their company to take greater actions on climate change, organized an internal petition for the September 20, 2019 "climate strike" walkout.

The walkout was inspired by the "Global Climate Strike," a student-led movement sparked by climate activist Greta Thunberg, a 16-year-old from Sweden. The Amazon climate group has previously called for more action from Amazon during its annual shareholder meeting and offered support for a Prime Day warehouse strike in Minnesota.

Amazon Employees For Climate Justice is demanding the company stop donating to politicians and lobbying groups who deny the existence of climate change, restrict its work with oil and gas companies, and cut down its carbon emissions to zero by 2030. The group, in addition to physical protests, has a growing online presence[1] that they use to share their thoughts and feelings about the company.

Asked whether Amazon supports the strike or would retaliate or support this protest, Amazon officials stated that "Amazon employees receive an allotment of paid time off every year, and they can use this time as they wish."[2]

While the walkout is tied to a broader climate strike, it serves as another example of employees speaking up for changes within their own companies and creating internal groups to do it. Other internal groups include Whole Worker (Whole Foods employees) and We Won't Build It (engineers fighting against Amazon's connections to US Immigration and Customs Enforcement).

Whether employees create established groups or not, management is going to have to deal with this rising tide of activism much the same way previous generations dealt with labor issues. They will have to walk

---

[1] Amazon Employees for Climate Justice. https://medium.com/@amazonemployeesclimatejustice, (accessed September 2019).
[2] C|net. 2019. "Hundreds of Amazon Employees Plan to Join Climate Change Strike." https://www.cnet.com/news/hundreds-of-amazon-employees-plan-to-join-climate-change-strike/, (accessed September 2019).

a fine line between following the demands of every individual or small numbers of employees or ignoring a major issue. Employers need to make sure employees _know_ that they have been heard, their concerns have been taken seriously (even if management does not change course), and that they are respected. Otherwise they risk disenfranchising their workforce.

(Some) Businesses Are Stepping Up

President Trump's decision to withdraw the United States from the Paris Agreement seems to have galvanized increasing support in the United States for the treaty. In response to that announcement more than 20 states and 50 cities pledged to follow the prevailing scientific wisdom and maintain—and in some cases, accelerate—their efforts.

Similarly, businesses that have been saying for years that "sustainability is a business strategy" are demonstrating that it is more than just words (being "politically correct" if you will). At the COP22 meeting in Marrakech, 365 companies and major investors reaffirmed their commitment to do their parts and asked government officials in the United States to continue efforts "to realize the Paris Agreement's commitment of a global economy that limits global temperature rise to well below 2 degrees Celsius."

When the automobile industry and oil and natural gas industries both reject efforts to roll back environmental standards (for mileage and methane emissions measurement and reporting, respectively), it is a sign that they recognize that long term those things matter and that there is nothing to be gained and much to be lost (including public goodwill, market share, and the environment) from going backward.

The Need to Rebuild the Global Economy as a Sustainable Economy

It seems like a circular argument to state that one of the forces encouraging sustainability is the need to build something sustainable, but the 2008 collapse of global financial markets, the increasing number of severe storms and weather events, wildfire seasons in California that now extend throughout the year, the #metoo protests, and other political destabilizations around the world all demonstrate the need to build something that will resist environmental, social, or economic catastrophe in the future.

We are living in a period of major disruption and changes. While some eagerly embraced the disruption, others found it to be terrifying. As in the past, this has given rise to a wave of populism: where politicians offer simple or simplistic solutions that provide a way for people who feel overcome by events to feel better and less threatened. Brexit, the rise of the far right in Europe, and President Trump are all riding the wave of uncertainty (and fear) that comes when events move faster than comfort zones.

It is important to recognize that those who advocate for globalism and a more outward and a more progressive approach to science, education, innovation, and the future often cite the benefits of these things. But for people who genuinely fear them, they are seen as frightening, daunting, intimidating, and dangerous.

Globalization is both awe-inspiring and terrifying depending on your perspective. The current wave of populism is fueled not by misunderstanding but rather a well-founded fear of globalization.

In his recent book *Thank You for Being Late*[3] Thomas L. Friedman (no relation) recounts how GE issued an online challenge to create a strong and lightweight bracket design for mounting an aircraft engine. One person in central Indonesia literally beat GE's in-house team of professional engineers, submitting a 3D printable design via the Internet. GE was able to use the file to 3D print prototypes, on the opposite side of the planet, and determined that the design worked and met all of their specifications. That is an amazing opportunity, if you happen to be the Indonesian designer, but also a threat if you are looking for a job at GE and suddenly have to compete with the best minds around the world for it.

When ideas come in across borders, time zones, and continents, one person sees them as sparks of inspiration leading to a better future, while

---

[3]T.L. Friedman. 2016. Thank You for Being Late: *An Optimist's Guide to Thriving in the Age of Accelerations* (New York, NY: Farrar, Straus and Giroux Publisher). https://www.amazon.com/Thank-You-Being-Late-Accelerations/dp/0374273537.

another views the same thing as economic "invasions" with the potential to destroy their present.

The desire to go back to an earlier, simpler time may feel comfortable but, in the end, progress cannot be stopped. Trade isolation and denial of "what's out there" never works and, in the digital age, will be even harder to contain. David Von Drehle explains in "Populism Is Doomed to Fail" (The Washington Post, October 12, 2019) that while "Complexity feeds populism; simplicity tends to cure it." He goes on:

> Populism can also be cured through competent, responsible leadership. The rise of today's populism cannot be blamed on demagogues alone. A measure of responsibility belongs to an entire generation of political leaders, thought leaders and cultural leaders who blithely celebrated disruption and change without enough concern for the wreckage. "Move fast and break things" was Facebook founder Mark Zuckerberg's motto, but it captured a spirit widely shared by elites. In their excitement and haste, they lost touch with those whose social contracts and hopes for the future were part of what was broken.[4]

Some people live under the flawed premise that well-being and wealth (and even jobs) are a "zero sum" proposition and that for one person to gain, another (or many others) has to lose. The fact is, those things are created and therefore do not need to be "redistributed" or "reallocated."

Wealth, like the jobs needed to generate it, is not finite—it is generated, created, and grown. Yes, there are shifts, such as those brought on by automation, and we've done a poor job at developing a flexible workforce that is able to take transferable skills to other industries or tasks, but job creation is not only possible, it is preferable.

We cannot close the door on globalization, whether we want to or not. It is here to stay. And it will carry on. What we must do is ensure that, like capitalism, the benefits are shared more equitably and that we

---

[4]D. Von Drehle. 2019. "Populism Is Doomed to Fail," The Washington Post. https://www.thehour.com/opinion/article/Populism-is-doomed-to-fail-14516777.php, (accessed October 14, 2019).

are not exhausting the planet's capacity to regenerate at an ever-increasing rate. The only solution is to focus less on individual and more on collective progress. This argues for a more responsible and sustainable business model, one that addresses peoples' environmental (climate change), social (including equal rights and opportunity, living wages, racial tensions, etc.), and governance concerns.

Discussion Questions

1. How do you feel about the concept of "lifelong learning?"
2. How does it change your feeling if it becomes a necessity rather than an option?

Challenges Facing Sustainability as a Business Model

Smaller Businesses Are Harder to Reach

Eco-Coach's Anca Novacovici cautions that while the larger and medium-sized organizations continue to come on board, smaller organizations, which employ most individuals around the world, have been more tentative for two main reasons: they are not as aware of the many benefits that sustainability can bring to their business and to their bottom line and they still have the perception that it costs a lot. "There is still a lot of education that needs to happen at the small business level."

Lack of Consensus on Standards

As we examined earlier, globally there is no real consensus on what sustainability and corporate responsibility are, or how they can be universally defined and applied across cultures. Sustainability provides the opportunity—and some would argue the obligation—to further issues such as human rights such as providing equal opportunity, living wages, and improved working conditions. It is quite natural, however, that those who have benefited from the status quo—governments, religious leaders, and economically powerful in those countries—would see the exact same actions as political agenda that is an attempt to destabilize local governments, faiths, and society. From this perspective, these businesses, through the fault of their own best intentions, are viewed with suspicion if not outright hostility.

The seemingly sensible strategy is one of falling back on regulatory compliance, linking social responsibility goals and objectives to cultural competence; and a desire to demonstrate respect for local cultures, customs, and laws. Following this model, as we have seen, not only does not make one a leader, it is increasingly seen as inadequate. Companies have found themselves facing outcry for engaging in what are perfectly acceptable practices overseas that offend the sensibility of shareholders and customers in their home country.

This can lead to a troubling situation when a company genuinely believes itself to be socially responsible yet finds itself suffering from criticism leveled by its stakeholders. When there is this kind of disagreement between an organization and its stakeholders over expectations, it becomes an imperative to reconcile. The shift can happen with stunning swiftness and many companies find themselves ill prepared when the perception changes. Wal-Mart, the world's largest retailer, enjoyed status as one of the world's most admired companies for years. Seemingly overnight the company was faced with strong criticism for its wages and employee benefits (both of which are well within industry norms) for not doing more to advance these issues. This despite an impressive focus on environmental sustainability; including the use of fuel-efficient trucks, working to reduce waste in both packaging and garbage, and pledging to become energy neutral.

Not surprisingly, there are efforts underway to quantify sustainability efforts and promote global standards. Groups such as the Global Reporting Initiative (GRI), a large multistakeholder network of thousands of experts in dozens of countries worldwide, have developed a popular, but not universally set of guidelines. The Dow Jones Sustainability Index, FTSE Index, UN Sustainable Development Goals, Paris Agreement, etc., are all efforts to define what which is universally agreed upon.

But until a set of standards emerge there will always be disconnects and confusion. Of course, companies would do well to ensure that their practices conform to local laws and regulations and engage proactively in stakeholder dialogue to ensure that they are keeping abreast and helping to manage stakeholder expectations.

As companies strive to define their own standards, transparency becomes the name of the game, as stakeholders who are brought into the process that defines company policies, commitments, practices, and goals. The company must set benchmarks and then hold themselves to those standards—reporting and announcing their actual results publicly.

Corporate Structures

Sustainability and corporate responsibility activities combine elements of strategic planning, human resources, environmental, legal, financial, ethics, risk management, communications, and a host of other functions. It is especially difficult to develop a program that provides value to all these various functions unless the organization is structured to facilitate and encourage cross-functional efforts.

Effective sustainability programs require local implementation of corporate-wide ideals. It is particularly difficult to coordinate in larger organizations that take pride in their corporate culture of decentralized decision-making. Sustainability also has no obvious home within traditional corporate structures. When the function exists as a separate entity, it may report to the CEO or chief operating officer. It is common to place sustainability within the legal/risk management functions, but it can also be found in human resources and communications. Where it lies often reveals the impetus behind the creation of the function, whether a strategic decision (i.e., a business that has identified its environmental impacts as most material) or based on individual executives' passions or abilities.

Companies that wish to have credible stakeholder communications must recognize a fundamental change back to the true meaning of the words "public" and "relations" since "stakeholders" really are the various "publics" who have a vested interest in your organization; and relationships are meaningful interactions (and not simply the delivery of corporate messages). This requires open and honest communications, with an implied compact between company and stakeholders that the company will eschew hyperbole and rhetoric provided the community is open to working with the company to work through (not around) issues.

Incentive and Reward Programs Based on Short-Term Results

A close relative of the structural impediments to implementing a strategic program is the fact that incentive and reward programs are often aligned with financial performance on a monthly, quarterly, and annual basis and do not take into consideration the value of long-term strategic approaches. Managers receiving incentive bonuses based on strong quarterly returns may be passively being discouraged from engaging in environmental or community programs that can be viewed as a cost. When Paul Polman announced that Unilever would no longer issue quarterly earnings reports, he explained:

> We needed to remove the temptation to work only toward the next set of numbers ... Better decisions are being made. We don't have discussions about whether to postpone the launch of a brand by a month or two or not to invest capital, even if investing is the right thing to do, because of quarterly commitments. We have moved to a more mature dialogue with our investor base.[5]

Culture of "Instant Gratification"

Americans are traditionally viewed as impatient and many have commented on the seeming obsession with "instant gratification." The concept of delayed gratification is a difficult one for a society that values fast food, "the fast buck," and in which the trappings of wealth are paraded nightly in the media. Those cultural values have been the dominant cultural overlay for capitalism in the 20th century. As the 21st century

---

[5]McKinsey. 2014. "Business, Society, and the Future of Capitalism." https://www.mckinsey.com/business-functions/sustainability/our-insights/business-society-and-the-future-of-capitalism, (accessed August 15, 2019).

approaches its one-quarter mark, the future of this cultural overlay is being called frequently into question.

In Conclusion

In boardrooms and executive suites around the world, business leaders—those people who are truly leading and not just managing their companies—are writing a new chapter of capitalism. The new chapter seeks to preserve (and expand) the gains in quality of life, longevity, health, well-being, and prosperity that are the best results of this economic system while working to ensure that those benefits are universally shared and they do not come at the expense of the Earth's vast, but finite, natural resources. These business leaders understand that these gaps threaten to reverse the gains that we have achieved.

The lifestyles we associate with development are massively resource intensive, and the benefits are not universally shared.

As was pointed out earlier, as a species we are collectively using far more natural resources than the Earth can replenish each year. And while more people are indeed living better than ever before, many millions are not. And we cannot simply produce more to 'fill the gap', nor can we increase the disparities in favor of preserving the environment.

When a system continues to produce the same results, one must conclude that the system, whether it was intended to produce those outcomes or not, is designed to produce those outcomes. Therefore, we must look at capitalism systemically, and not just tinker around the edges.

For those who question whether capitalism itself is fundamentally at odds with a vision for corporate responsibility and a sustainable future, it is well worth to remember that capitalism has brought those benefits to more people than any other economic system conceived or tried. We must preserve those gains by keeping the elements that have driven successes while learning and applying the lessons from the past to develop a more sustainable and more equitable model for the 21st century.

This new model of sustainable capitalism is seeking to align performance of the private sector in harmony with the progress of society and with the Earth's capacity to generate resources.

"We're sitting on this goldmine; this wonderful instrument called capitalism," explains Indra Nooyi, former CEO of PepsiCo.[6] "Let's really write the next chapter, so that we don't read these articles about inequality and environmental issues and just sit back and do nothing about it."

> The next chapter will be written by all of us; the next generation of executives, subject matter experts, academics and investors, commentators, regulators, non-profit leaders. Everybody has to come together to write this next chapter of capitalism. This next chapter cannot be written by just one person, one institution or one sector because the goal of capitalism is to create value ... financial, societal, scientific or otherwise ... for everyone in society. We know that value is there. We need to build a sustainable future.

This is a sentiment that comes from a sense of legacy, something one often sees in family-owned businesses (or businesses where the founder remains a spiritual if not physical presence within the organization). In these companies the idea of stewarding something that was built and passed to them, and that they will one day pass down to subsequent generations, may come more naturally. But for leaders who are often in the C-suite for tenures measured (and rewarded) in months, it may be hard to have this mind-set.

But it is encouraging to see, increasingly, business leaders do have this mind-set. It is evident in the number of American companies that have pledged to "stay in" the Paris Agreement. While it may seem that we have taken—and are taking—giant steps backward, it is important to remember that evolution happens when new traits are more suitable for a changing environment. Our social, political, economic environments are also undergoing their own versions of "climate change."

As Darwin explained, a changing environment (or environments) leads to the survival of the most adaptable. The imperatives for change are clear and all around us.

---

[6]J. Friedman. 2014. "Writing Capitalism's New Chapter." https://www.huffpost.com/entry/writing-capitalisms-new-c_b_6187056, (accessed August 15, 2019).

Discussion Questions

1. Is capitalism inherently unsustainable?

2. How has your thinking evolved over the course of reading this book? Has it?

Key Resources

Chapter 1—Introduction: Corporate Sustainability

1. Report: US EIA. 2019. "EIA Forecasts Renewables Will Be Fastest Growing Source of Electricity Generation." https://www.eia.gov/todayinenergy/detail.php?id=38053.
2. Article: Karak, M. 2019,. "Climate Change and Syria's Civil War," *JSTOR Daily*. https://daily.jstor.org/climate-change-and-syrias-civil-war/.
3. Article: Pond, E. 1984. "East Germany Disputes Its Status as the Most Polluted Country in Europe," *Christian Science Monitor*. https://www.csmonitor.com/1984/1005/100538.html.
4. Article: Chapman, S. 1990. "Poverty, Hunger and Other Evils of Communism," *Chicago Tribune*. https://www.chicagotribune.com/news/ct-xpm-1990-01-25-9001070410-story.html.

Chapter 2—Integrating Sustainability into the Business

1. Book: Friedman, M. 1962. *Capitalism and Freedom*. Chicago, IL: University of Chicago Press. https://www.press.uchicago.edu/ucp/books/book/chicago/C/bo18146821.html.
2. Article: Murray, A. 2019. "America's CEOs Seek a New Purpose for the Corporation," *Fortune*. https://fortune.com/longform/business-roundtable-ceos-corporations-purpose/.
3. Visser, W. 2019. "Integrated Value Management: Implementing Sustainable Transformation." *AMS Sustainable Transformation Briefing Series*, no. 5, Antwerp Management School. http://www.waynevisser.com/articles.
4. Book: Young, S. 2003. *Moral Capitalism*. San Francisco, CA: Berrett-Koehler Publishers, pp. 175–76. https://www.penguinrandomhouse.com/books/574689/moral-capitalism-by-stephen-young/.
5. Press Release: Unilever. October 5, 2018. "Unilever's Sustainable Living Plan Continues to Fuel Growth." https://www.unilever.com/news/press-releases/2018/unilevers-sustainable-living-plan-continues-to-fuel-growth.html.
6. Report: PwC. 2011. "Millennials at Work." https://www.pwc.de/de/prozessoptimierung/assets/millennials-at-work-2011.pdf.

7. Book: Wu, J., G. Lodorfos, A. Dean, and G. Gioulmpaxiotisb. 2015. "The Market Performance of Socially Responsible Investment during Periods of the Economic Cycle—Illustrated Using the Case of FTSE. Managerial and Decision Economics." https://doi.org/10.1002/mde.2772.

8. Article: Brown, A. 2019. "Sustainable Investing At All-Time High, Says Morgan Stanley," *Triple Pundit*. https://www.triplepundit.com/story/2019/sustainable-investing-all-time-high-says-morgan-stanley/84916/?fbclid=IwAR1Vc6z-xxEHT2M6-VZ_gyjgo0gV27oOSMHXTQu2k4M3noGm3jXeNw1K8xc.

9. Book: Monks, R., and A.R. Lajoux. *Corporate Valuation for Portfolio Investment: Analyzing Assets, Earnings, Cash Flow, Stock Price, Governance, and Special Situations*. Hoboken, NJ: Bloomberg Press. https://www.amazon.com/Corporate-Valuation-Portfolio-Investment-Governance/dp/1576603172.

10. Article: Bloomberg. August 7, 2019. "Big Money Starts to Dump Stocks That Pose Climate Risks," https://www.bloomberg.com/news/articles/2019-08-07/big-money-starts-to-dump-stocks-that-pose-climate-risks.

11. Press Release: August 12, 2019. "Socially Responsible Investing and ESG: It's Not Just a Millennial Trend." https://www.businesswire.com/news/home/20190812005374/en/.

Chapter 3—Five Keys to Integrate Sustainability into the Business

1. Book: Shultzs, H. 2012. *Onward: How Starbucks Fought for Its Life without Losing Its Soul*. New York, NY: Rodale Books. https://www.amazon.com/Onward-Starbucks-Fought-without-Losing/dp/1609613821.

2. Article: Welch, J. 2015. "Winning, Do You Have a Jerk Employee Problem? How to Deal with It." https://jackwelch.strayer.edu/winning/jerk-employee-problem.

3. Article: Global Strategy Group. 2016. "Business & Politics Do They Mix?" http://www.globalstrategygroup.com/wp-content/uploads/2016/12/2016-GSG-Business-and-Politics_Do-They-Mix_Fourth-Annual-Study.pdf.

Chapter 4—Creating a Leading Program

1. Press Release: WGL Holdings. 2016. "Washington Gas Exceeds Carbon Reduction Goals Four Years Ahead of Schedule." http://sustainability.wglholdings.com/blog/washington-gas-exceeds-carbon-reduction-goals-four-years-ahead-schedule.

2. Publication: UPS. 2019. "Environmental Responsibility." https://sustainability.ups.com/sustainability-strategy/environmental-responsibility.

3. Publication: UPS. 2018. "Goals and Progress: 2018: Progress Toward Our Aspirations." https://sustainability.ups.com/progress-report/goals-and-progress/.

4. Article: Morgan, J. 2018. "Inside the UPS Rolling Laboratory," *Fleet Equipment.* https://www.fleetequipmentmag.com/the-rolling-laboratory/.

5. Website: Beumelburg, C. 2016. "Breakthrough Technology for Carbon Capture." https://www.heidelbergcement.com/en/leilac-research-project.

6. Article: Mohin, T. 2019. "Supply Chain Transparency Is a Business Necessity." https://medium.com/@GlobalReportingInitiative/supply-chain-transparency-is-a-business-necessity-b88451a9a6ef.

7. Report: Unilever. 2011. "Inspiring Sustainable Living: Expert Insights into Consumer Behavior and Unilever's Five Levers for Change." https://www.unilever.com/Images/slp_5-levers-for-change_tcm244-414399_en.pdf.

Chapter 5—How Sustainability Is Changing Traditional Functions of Business

1. Website: Reputation Institute. 2018. "Corporate Social Responsibility—Align Perception with Reality." https://insights.reputationinstitute.com/blog-ri/corporate-social-responsibility-align-perception-with-reality.

2. Website: Reputation Institute. 2018. "Companies with an Excellent Reputation Perform Better and Are Insulated Against Failure." https://www.reputationinstitute.com/solutions.

3. Report: Cone Communications. 2016. "Millennial Employee Engagement Study." https://static1.squarespace.com/static/56b4a7472b8dde3df5b7013f/t/5819e8b303596e3016ca0d9c/1478092981243/2016+Cone+Communications+Millennial+Employee+Engagement+Study_Press+Release+and+Fact+Sheet.pdf.

4. Article: Pelosi, P. 2019. "Millennials Want Workplaces with Social Purpose. How Does Your Company Measure Up?" https://www.chieflearningofficer.com/2018/02/20/millennials-want-workplaces-social-purpose-company-measure/.

5. Article: Dwyer, P. 2015. "The Myth of Shareholder Value," *Bloomberg.* https://www.bloomberg.com/opinion/articles/2015-05-11/shareholder-value-isn-t-the-only-way-to-run-a-successful-company.

6. Book: Rangan, S. October, 2015. *Essays on Capitalism, Business, and Society, Rangan, Subramanian, Performance and Progress.* Oxford, UK: Oxford University Press. https://www.amazon.com/Performance-Progress-Capitalism-Business-Society/dp/0198744285.

7. Report: Shelton Group. 2018. "Social Purpose Is the New Black." https://storage.googleapis.com/shelton-group/Pulse%20Reports/Brands%20%26%20Stands%20-%20Final%20Report%202018.pdf.

8. Report: CVS Health. 2015. "Cigarettes Out. Health In. An analysis of the rebrand of CVS Health." https://communication.depaul.edu/about/news-and-events/2015/Documents/ArthurPageSocietyAwards15/PageCVSStudy15.pdf.

9. Article: Fromm, J. 2019. "Brands Still Matter, If They're Fueled by Purpose." https://www.forbes.com/sites/jefffromm/2019/07/11/brands-still-matter-if-theyre-fueled-by-purpose/#3486eeba3b0a.

10. Article: Schiavone, L. September 13, 2019. "The Time Has Come to Talk About Oysters," *LA Review of Books*. https://lareviewofbooks.org/article/the-time-has-come-to-talk-about-oysters/.

11. Article: Kolowich, L. 2014. "Delighting People in 140 Characters: An Inside Look at JetBlue's Customer Service Success," *Hubspot*. https://blog.hubspot.com/marketing/jetblue-customer-service-twitter.

Chapter 6—What's Next?

1. Article: Amazon Employees for Climate Justice. https://medium.com/@amazonemployeesclimatejustice.

2. Article: C|net. 2019. "Hundreds of Amazon Employees Plan to Join Climate Change Strike." https://www.cnet.com/news/hundreds-of-amazon-employees-plan-to-join-climate-change-strike/.

3. Book: Friedman, T.L. 2016. *Thank You for Being Late: An Optimist's Guide to Thriving in the Age of Accelerations*. New York, NY: Farrar, Straus and Giroux Publisher. https://www.amazon.com/Thank-You-Being-Late-Accelerations/dp/0374273537.

4. Article: D. Von Drehle. 2019. "Populism Is Doomed to Fail," *The Washington Post*. https://www.thehour.com/opinion/article/Populism-is-doomed-to-fail-14516777.php.

5. Report: McKinsey. 2014. "Business, Society, and the Future of Capitalism." https://www.mckinsey.com/business-functions/sustainability/our-insights/business-society-and-the-future-of-capitalism.

About the Author

With an international career spanning three decades, *John Friedman* is an award-winning communications professional and recognized sustainability expert who has helped some of the leading global companies to integrate their operational, financial, and cultural aspirations into sustainable and responsible business practices. He has been instrumental in helping three companies—Lafarge, Sodexo, and WGL Holdings—rise to the top of the sustainability rankings (Dow Jones Sustainability Indices/RobecoSAM and MSCI) for their respective sectors: building materials, food service/facilities management, and energy. He has helped define long-range targets including science-based targets, developed and tracked annual goals in support of those targets, as well as managed programs relating to environmental stewardship, social progress, and sound governance practices.

Friedman is a founder and served on the board for the Sustainable Business Network of Washington (SBNOW), which was one of the first, and grew to be the largest, SBNs in the country. He is a respected voice for sustainability, often presenting at colleges and universities as well as meetings and conferences including Sustainable Brands, 3BLForum, Just Means, and Business for Social Responsibility (BSR). He has also authored more than 150 articles that have been published by Reuters, Huffington Post Business, Sustainable Brands, Triple Pundit, and others. On digital media, @JohnFriedman is recognized as a thought leader; he is on Triple Pundit's List of the Top 30 Sustainability Bloggers on Twitter, #3 on GreenBiz list of most influential "twitterati," #14 on Guardian Business' 30 most influential sustainability voices in America, voted #4 of the "100 leading voices in CSR" by Global CEO Magazine readers, and has regularly been included among the top voices in CSR by Forbes' Brandfog.

Friedman has a communications degree from Albany State University and business certification from Duke University's Fuqua School of Business.

LinkedIn: https://www.linkedin.com/in/johnfriedman
E-mail: JohnFriedmanCSR@gmail.com

Index

OTHER TITLES IN OUR ENVIRONMENTAL AND SOCIAL SUSTAINABILITY FOR BUSINESS ADVANTAGE COLLECTION

Robert Sroufe, Duquesne University, *Editor*

- *ISO 50001 Energy Management Systems: What Managers Need to Know About Energy and Business Administration* by Johannes Kals
- *Developing Sustainable Supply Chains to Drive Value, Volume I: Management Issues, Insights, Concepts, and Tools—Foundations* by Robert P. Sroufe
- *Developing Sustainable Supply Chains to Drive Value, Volume II: Management Issues, Insights, Concepts, and Tools—Implementation* by Robert Sroufe
- *Social Development Through Benevolent Business* by Kaylan Sankar Mandal
- *Climate Change Management: Special Topics in the Context of Asia* by Thi Thu Huong Ha
- *Human Resource Management for Organizational Sustainability* by Radha R. Sharma

Announcing the Business Expert Press Digital Library

Concise e-books business students need for classroom and research

This book can also be purchased in an e-book collection by your library as

- *a one-time purchase,*
- *that is owned forever,*
- *allows for simultaneous readers,*
- *has no restrictions on printing, and*
- *can be downloaded as PDFs from within the library community.*

Our digital library collections are a great solution to beat the rising cost of textbooks. E-books can be loaded into their course management systems or onto students' e-book readers.
The **Business Expert Press** digital libraries are very affordable, with no obligation to buy in future years. For more information, please visit **www.businessexpertpress.com/librarians**.
To set up a trial in the United States, please email **sales@businessexpertpress.com**.

CPSIA information can be obtained
at www.ICGtesting.com
Printed in the USA
FSHW021833061020
74472FS